The Encyclopedia
of
Immaturity

by the editors of

KLUTZ®

KLUTZ

creates activity books and other great stuff for kids ages 3 to 103. We began our corporate life in 1977 in a garage we shared with a Chevrolet Impala. Although we've outgrown that first office, Klutz galactic headquarters remains in Palo Alto, California, and we're still staffed entirely by real human beings. For those of you who collect mission statements, here's ours:

· Create wonderful things · Be good · Have fun

Write Us

We would love to hear your comments regarding this or any of our books. We have many!

KLUTZ®

450 Lambert Avenue
Palo Alto, CA 94306 USA

Book manufactured in Taiwan. 85

Distributed in the UK by Scholastic UK Ltd Westfield Road, Southam, Warwickshire England CV47 0RA

Distributed in Australia by Scholastic Australia Ltd PO Box 579, Gosford, NSW Australia 2250

Distributed in Canada by Scholastic Canada Ltd 604 King Street West, Toronto, Ontario Canada M5V 1E1

ISBN-10: 1-59174-427-X
ISBN-13: 978-1-59174-427-6

4

Visit Our Website

You can check out all the stuff we make, find a nearby retailer, request a catalog, sign up for a newsletter, e-mail us or just goof off!

www.klutz.com

Introduction

The information in this volume was gathered over the course of a misspent and lifelong childhood. The sources were extremely diverse and, given the long time frame, many of them will have to remain nameless. In most cases they would probably insist on it anyway. The outstanding exception is our longtime hero, Martin Gardner, a magic buff, mathematician, teacher and philosopher, whose vast brain and experience encompass a great deal more than everything in this book.

We didn't realize it at the time, but we started this project in 1977, when we published our first title, a book called *Juggling for the Complete Klutz*. Juggling was the only thing we could do at the time that people were willing to watch, and publishing a book about it seemed like a harmless way to postpone a real job and the whole growing-up thing.

That was more than a few books ago and we've had to learn a lot of new things in the course of making them all. Fortunately, despite many years' worth of excellent opportunities, growing up was never one of them.

And that's what this book is all about.

John Cassidy
Palo Alto, CA

Table of Contents

The Klutz
maturity quiz

How Old Are You Really?

You actually have two ages: One, your "birthday age," which you can get by counting the years since you were born, and two, your real age, which you can get by taking this maturity test and then adding (or subtracting) a maturity factor from your birthday age.

❑ Y   **Have you ever replaced the toilet paper**
❑ N   **without being told?**

❑ Y   **Do you think cereal that makes your milk**
❑ N   **turn chocolate is a bad thing?**

❑ Y   **Do you think it's unsafe**
❑ N   **to walk up the slide?**

❑ Y   **Can you give someone an underdog**
❑ N   **in class, if they're sitting in front of you?**

❑ Y   **Can you get a noogie in**
❑ N   **a sandwich?**

❑ Y   **How about a wedgie?**
❑ N

❑ Y   **When you roast marshmallows, are**
❑ N   **you OK with either brown or black?**

❑ Y   **Do you know what IRS**
❑ N   **stands for?**

SCORING

Each "yes" or "don't know" is worth +1 year.

Each "no" is worth –1 year.

Can You Walk Funny?

You probably already know how to do a regular walk. But if you're reading this book, you're probably not a regular person, and that's why you should perfect your own funny walk.

The photographs here should serve as inspiration. Your own funny walk should be uniquely yours. Good luck. If you're reading this book, we have confidence in you.

Anybody else feel a breeze?

Ear Wiggling Made Easy

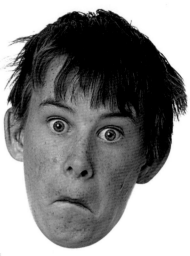

1 Use adhesive bandages to attach a string to the back of your ears.

2 Tie another string to the middle of the first one. Let it dangle down through the back of your shirt.

3 Pull on the aforementioned string while standing in front of a group of people.

Pull on string. Don't tell anyone you're doing this.

> ...az etelbol amit nekem kinalsz, vagyen vagyok az elso?

Evett Mar Valaki Ebbol...

OK, parents, put away your books. Today's foreign language quiz is in Hungarian. Read the sample phrase out loud, translate it, and then check off the correct box. Good luck to everyone!

❑ Hello, friend! You have taken off your socks and now I can no longer breathe.

❑ Waiter, this meal you're serving me, am I the first to eat it?

❑ Take me to your leader, Mr. Earth Person, and check the tires on my spaceship.

❑ Madam, is this your wolverine that has become ill on my shoe?

Answer in back.

The nastiest activity in this book

How to Fake a Sneeze!

1 Wet your hand under a faucet.

2 Stand behind someone (maybe you're in line?) and fake the sound of a huge, sloppy sneeze. Simultaneously, shake the water on your hand onto the back of their neck.

3 When they turn around, say "Bless Me!" and sniffle a few times. Smile.

How to Skip Stones

There's a magic angle in stone skipping of about 20 degrees. If you throw a hard sidearm with a good flattish stone, and the stone hits the water with its front edge lifted up at 20 degrees, you should get 8 or 9 skips pretty regularly. The pro's can get over 30, but that has to do with sheer power, the right angle and a perfect stone. If it's too flat, like a small Frisbee®, it will start to slice between skips and that will throw your angle off just enough.

20 degrees

1 Throw a hard sidearm…

2 …with a lot of spin.

3 And lift the edge 20 degrees. Don't hit the water flat.

REFINNEJ

BOCAJ

ERALC

What's Your Eman?

DARB

ADNALOY

Write your name on a piece of paper. Then, write it backwards. This is your eman. Learn it well and practice the pronunciation. Then, the next time your parents want you to meet one of their boring grown-up friends, turn around, put your hand out behind you, shake theirs backwards and say, for example, *"How do you do, my eman is Ekim."* This almost guarantees that they will never ask you to meet one of their friends again.

EKIM

NIVEK

How to Read Grown-Up Minds

Ask the nearest grown-up the following questions. Tell them it's part of an important nationwide survey and thank them for participating.

1 "Think of some country that starts with D. Don't tell me what it is."
(Typical grown-up will think: *Denmark*.)

2 "Take the last letter of that country and think of any animal that starts with it. Again, don't tell me what it is."
(Typical grown-up will think: *kangaroo*.)

3 "Take the last letter of that animal and think of a fruit that starts with it. Don't say anything, just think."
(Typical grown-up will think: *orange*.)

4 Finally, put your hand on their forehead, close your eyes, and say the following:
"Orange… you're thinking of an orange."

Typical grown-up

The Best Knock-Knock Joke Ever Told

There are 1,264,112 knock-knock jokes in the world. Only one of them is funny. Here it is.

A "u-draw-it" page

Explorer Discovers New Breed of Snapping Crocodile

O rville T. Snacktime, renowned African explorer, is shown here on a recent expedition to the headwaters of the River Watchyourbutt. Orville was attempting to get to the bottom of an ancient African legend about a huge, ugly killer crocodile. Orville achieved a startling dual success: At the exact moment he was able to get to the bottom of the legend, the legend was able to get to the bottom of him.

Add drawing
of crocodile
here.

How to Make Noises Under Your Arm

Learning how to make rude noises under your arm can lead to a better life, a better job, higher pay and more friends. Or at least different friends. To learn the basics, just follow the photographic instructions, but be aware that there is greatness out there for those who choose to pursue it. A guy in Texas can do the University of Texas fight song under his arm and if you go onto the Web (we were too frightened) you might be able to find achievements even more dazzling.

1

Identify which hand you're going to use.

2

Cup it.

3

Insert...

4

...under arm.

5

Lift and…

6

…squeeze.

7

Lift and…

8

…squeeze. Repeat.

How to Do an Ollie

This is the basic skateboard trick. It's how you get your first air. Unfortunately, you won't get it on your first try. Or your second, either. In fact, it takes days of practice before it begins to even semi-work. And the pro's will tell you they're still perfecting it after years of practice. But on the other hand, you can't be a real skateboarder without an ollie. It's the first rung up the ladder.

Start with one foot at the very tip of your tail, the other foot centered. Then get ready to…

…launch. Bend your knees deep and hit the power button.

The board should come off the ground. The challenge will be to keep it controlled, flat and directly under your feet. This won't come easy, but here are the points to remember.

Practice on a lawn to start, since you'll be falling a lot. Wear a helmet, wrist guards and knee pads.

Like so much of life, it's all about timing, getting your weight right and getting your feet to slide into place at just the right instant. Practice, practice, practice.

Your front foot has to stay in touch with the board. Check out the illustration for the technique. Your front foot kind of "rolls" up the board, keeping it flat, staying in touch.

When you top out (and that probably means about 2 inches at first), straighten your legs and get ready to land.

If you've put it all together, you'll "stick it" — centered, balanced and in control.

Connect the dots

A Vocab Quiz for Your Parents

O K, kids, time to get those parents of yours up to speed. Parents in other countries always test better than parents here, and we think it's because they're not getting tested enough. Connect the right definition with the right word.

Defenestrate •   • **possessing a big shapely rear end**

Callipygian •   • **fossilized dinosaur doo-doo**

Sternutate •   • **to go, depart the premises in a hurry**

Coprolite •   • **an unethical individual, frequently a politician**

Philtrum •   • **loose-fitting pants**

Snollygoster •   • **the little groove that runs between your upper lip and nose**

Galligaskins •   • **to throw out of a window**

Absquatulate •   • **sneeze**

See back for answers.

RUGREST

MODERN EAT

SIN IN COWS

Bumper sticker jumble

How'd You Like to Go to Odorcola State?

Or how about the U of Tinnesoma? Or Amabala? Or maybe just visit the great state of Meani? There are exactly one zillion ways to play our new game we call Bumper Sticker Jumble. All you need is a pair of scissors and the sticker from your local school.

SNODFART
UNIVERSITY

P.S. Each of these stickers is from a real school. Can you identify? See back for answers.

FRIED CALF

HAM ICING

SCARYUSE

Set a world record
Dot-to-Dots
for *Speed*

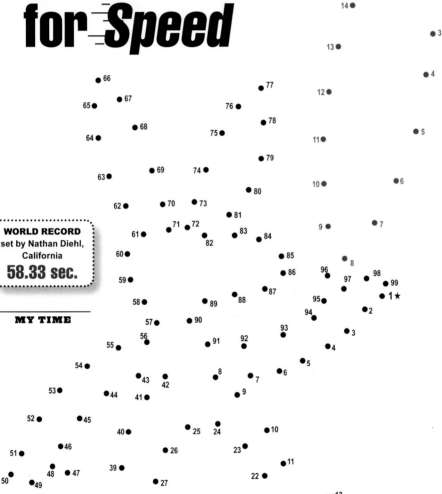

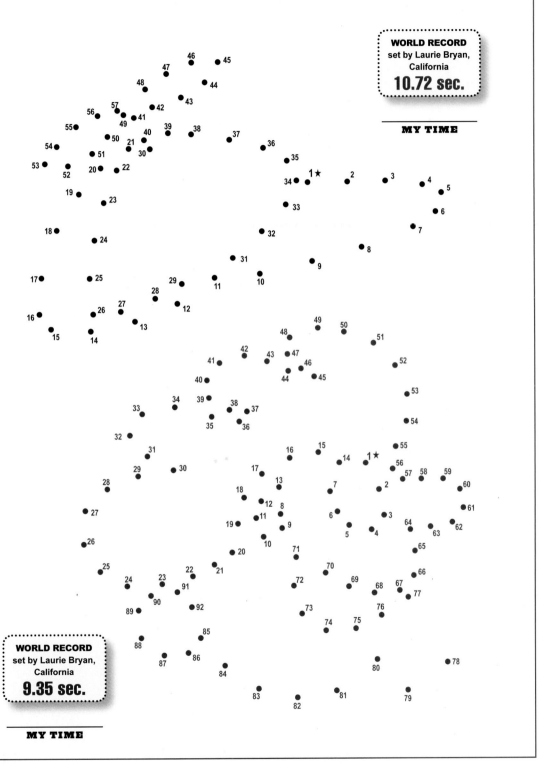

Headless Halloween

As you would expect, taking your head off and tucking it under one arm takes a bit of time, but there's no question it's worth every minute. The final effect will just about take your breath away.

Try this suggestion: Start working on this outfit about an hour before dad and mom are due home, then plant yourself on the couch. Just imagine their surprise and delight when they walk through the door!

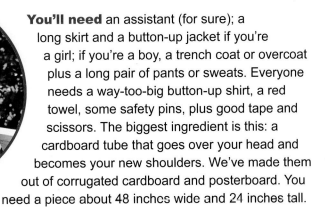

You'll need an assistant (for sure); a long skirt and a button-up jacket if you're a girl; if you're a boy, a trench coat or overcoat plus a long pair of pants or sweats. Everyone needs a way-too-big button-up shirt, a red towel, some safety pins, plus good tape and scissors. The biggest ingredient is this: a cardboard tube that goes over your head and becomes your new shoulders. We've made them out of corrugated cardboard and posterboard. You need a piece about 48 inches wide and 24 inches tall.

Warning It's hard to fake this with thin posterboard or soft cardboard. Use stout materials here.

1 If you're using corrugated cardboard, make sure the ribs run up the 24-inch side. (It doesn't have to be a new piece — you can flatten an old carton — previous folds don't matter.) Make your cardboard flexible by rolling it into a very tight roll.

Head goes in here.

Cut up a big cardboard box to make this.

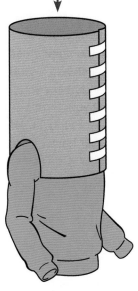

At least 3 inches

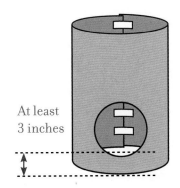

2 Roll your cardboard into a big tube (use plenty of tape). Put it on, mark where to cut for the head and shoulders, then take it off and do the cutting. Go back and forth a few times. Be picky.

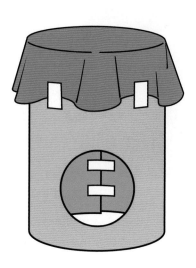

3 Cover the top of the tube with the red towel and pin or tape it in place.

4 Have your assistant place the tube on you. Make sure it fits and doesn't slump over to one side. Poke your head all the way through the hole and smile. This is the key. Make a solid-fitting tube!

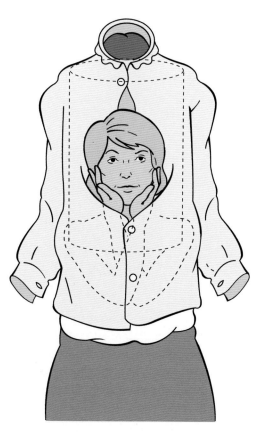

5 Next, put on the too-big shirt. Pull it over the tube and tuck it into your pants or skirt (I told you it had to be big) and stick your head through the unbuttoned front. Your assistant should button the shirt above and below your head. Now stick just your hands — not your arms — through the shirt front. Cross your hands under your chin, thumbs out. Don't let any of your arm show.

6 Then get into your too-long pants or skirt. Pull the waist up way high — to your armpits.

7 **For the girls:** Put the jacket on over the shirt. Stuff the sleeves with crumpled newspaper and safety pin them under your chin so it looks like your hands are coming out of the sleeves.*

For the boys: The trench coat goes on now. Stuff the sleeves with crumpled newspaper and pin them into place so it looks like your hands are coming out of them and tenderly holding your head.*

8 **Everybody's last step:** Your assistant makes the final adjustments, arranging everything so it looks just so. If you've made a good solid tube, you can walk all over the neighborhood with this costume.

*You can pin gloves in the sleeves if you want to leave your hands free.

Cut and tape

Bumper Stickers for People Who Don't Have Cars

How're My Manners?
1-800-YOU'RENOONETOTALK

I'd Rather Be Driving

Stick to back of shoe.

How's My Walking?
1-800-ASIFICAREDWHATYOUTHINK

Stick to back of shoe.

END BLASTING ZONE

WIDE LOAD

WIDE LOAD

Pretend This ➡ Is a Tablecloth

Next, place a coin where it says, and put the paper and the coin on your finger. Count to three and jerk out the strip. If you're smooth, quick, lucky and have been really good lately — the coin won't move. It will stay right there on your fingertip.

An additional challenge: If you can get your parents to allow you to try the real tablecloth trick, with all the silverware and dishes, e-mail us and we will send your parents our official **Coolest Parents in the World** certificate.

Grab.

Pull.

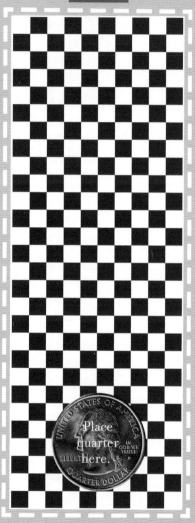

Place quarter here.

Cut out this tablecloth.

Quarter is supposed to stay put.

Paper strip

x

Grab here and jerk.

After you're dead
Cool Things to Do

- **Go to outer space!** Book a flight with Space Services of Houston, Texas. You'll travel on a privately launched SpaceX Falcon 1 rocket. Tickets cost somewhere between $995 and $5300 (one way). Restrictions? You have to be dead already, and your ashes have to fit inside a small stainless steel canister.

- **Fight crime!** The University of Tennessee Medical Center in Knoxville accepts full body donations. They are placed outdoors under controlled climate conditions so C.S.I. scientists can see what happens over various lengths of time.

- **Get engaged!** The people at LifeGem, in Chicago, Illinois, will extract the carbon from your cremated remains and turn it into a diamond engagement ring using an industrial press and extremely high temperatures. Takes about 4 months.

- **Just chill out.** The people at Alcor Life Extension Foundation in Scottsdale, Arizona, will store your body under extremely cold temperatures so no decay takes place. Then, in a couple of thousand years, when they figure out how to bring frozen dead bodies back to life, you'll be baaaaaack!

Throw Away Your Money!

Doug Stillinger showed us this one. Doug is a black belt in paper airplane design and the author of *The Klutz Book of Paper Airplanes,* the definitive work on the subject. Here is his design for the dollar bill dart. *Ingredients:* one dollar bill.

1 Start with George on top.

2 Fold in half.

3 Press down hard on the crease to make it perfect.

4 Unfold.

5 Fold in the corners.

6 Fold again to make a sharper nose.

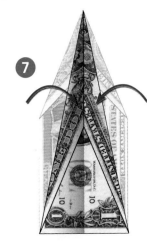

7 Fold one more time to make a super-sharp nose.

Turn over

8 Turn over and end up like this.

9 Fold in half. *Keep reading.*

10 See the dotted line?

11 Fold on it to make the wings.

Turn over

12 Turn over to look like this.

13 Unfold so the wings and body make a Y shape when you look at it from the back.

14 **Very important:** Pinch the back of each wing and bend upward.

You can also use a bigger bill if you're that kind of spender.

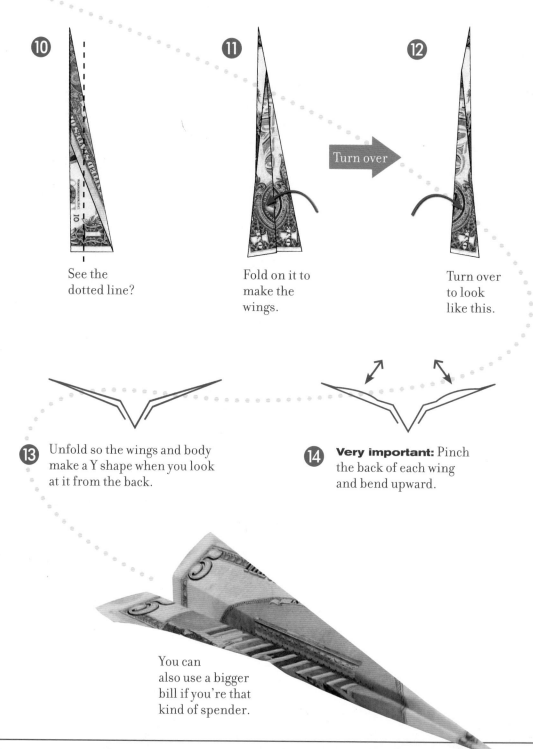

Be the first!

Can You Do a "Q"?

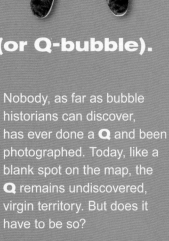

Bubblegum pro's refer to multiple bubbles this way:

The Single.

The Double.
Blowing one bubble inside the other.

The Triple.
Blowing two bubbles inside the first.

And the fabled Quad (or Q-bubble).
Blowing three bubbles inside the first.

I BLEW A Q

Date

Location

Your Name Here

Nobody, as far as bubble historians can discover, has ever done a **Q** and been photographed. Today, like a blank spot on the map, the **Q** remains undiscovered, virgin territory. But does it have to be so?

If you are able to blow a Q, put your name here on this certificate. Put in wallet. Carry for the rest of your life with pride.

Another "u-draw-it" page

Finalists in the World's Ugliest Tie Contest

Get out your markers and decorate these ties!

Another "u-draw-it" page

Meet the
Man-Eating
Goldfish

Get out your pen or pencil and put in the goldfish-a-zilla.

How to keep the seat next to you empty

Frequent Flier Tips

As you know, in today's crowded skies, getting a seat with an empty seat next to you takes a pretty big dose of luck.

At least it used to.

1. Get on board early, before the seat next to you gets occupied.

2. Sit down. Roll up a napkin and insert the end of it in nose.

3. Lean back and close eyes.

4. When they close the doors, you may open your eyes. Our guarantee? If there is only one empty seat on the whole plane, it will be the one next to you.

Yuck!

How Do You Say "Poop" in Potsdam?

People in Potsdam speak German, so "poop" translates to "bals." If you cross the border in Poland, say "kukor," which, by the way, is the most common word for poop around the world. Use it whenever you're abroad and in doubt.

But for those times you're not in a "caca" or "kukor" country, here's a handy tip sheet for travelers.

HERE'S HOW TO SAY POOP IN:

Icelandic: kúkur
German: bais
Hindi: tatti
Bengali: hagu
Japanese: unchi
Tagalog (Philippines): takla
Slovene: drek
Mandarin: da bien
Australian/N.Z.: poo
Korean: ddong
Arabic (Palestinian): assayir
Farsi (Iran): aiee
Lwu (East Africa): cet
West African languages: bino, wena or bangira

How to Kick a Toilet Plunger Field Goal

Set a toilet plunger on the floor two feet in front of the fridge. Your mother might like it to be clean. We don't care.

In either case, wind up and kick the plunger on the rubber part. Your goal is to stick the thing to the door. This won't happen the first time. If it did, it wouldn't be so special. But after just a few minutes of practice...

2 ft.

Did you ever wonder?

Are Your Friends Alive?

Photocopy this page, then cut along the dotted line, and dangle this reflex-checking strip of paper in the air.

1. Get your victim to hold thumb and forefinger on either side of the strip without touching it, right where it says *Victim's Finger*. Remember, no touching.

2. Without any warning, drop the strip.

3. Note where they catch it. If they fail to catch it at all, check for a pulse.

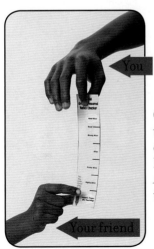

Get your victim to put their fingers over this strip. NO TOUCHING! And don't give them any warning.

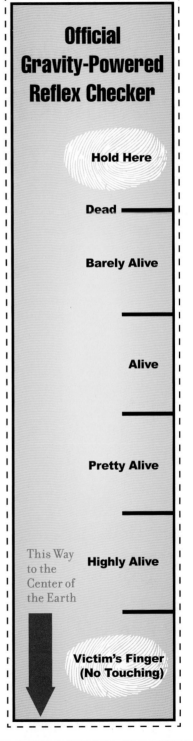

Official Gravity-Powered Reflex Checker

Hold Here

Dead

Barely Alive

Alive

Pretty Alive

This Way to the Center of the Earth

Highly Alive

Victim's Finger (No Touching)

What color are
Blender Burgers?

If you could travel to your stomach with a flashlight, what would you see? To find out, toss a Big Mac®, Coke® and fries into a blender and give it a whirl! We did! And we even drank some.

What color was it, do you think?

**Blender Burger
Color Quiz:**
Check the correct box.

 ❑ **A**

 ❑ **B**

 ❑ **C**

 ❑ **D**

 ❑ **E**

See back of the book for answers.

Set the World Record in Coin Flipping

Rules: Flip a coin until you get either heads or tails five times straight.

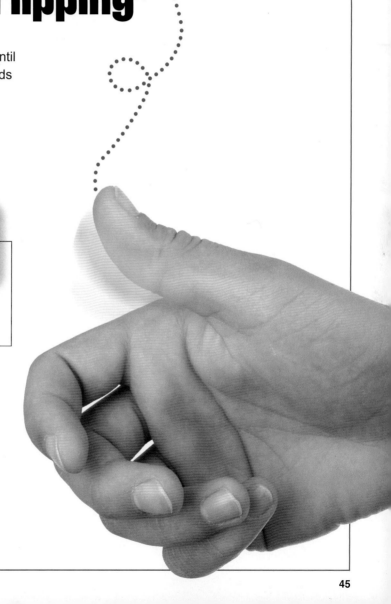

WORLD RECORD
set by Mary Pat Plottner, California

72 sec.

_____

MY TIME

*Another
"u-draw-it"
page*

Draw a
Giraffe

Get out your pencil or pen
and finish this portrait.

Extra credit: What would a
giraffe look like with a beach
ball stuck in its throat?

A "home-o-lympics" event

Set the World Record in Finger Snapping

Rules: Snap your fingers 24 times. One hand. If you can beat our record, e-mail us and if we believe it, we'll e-mail you a certificate of *World Finger Snapping Greatness.*

WORLD RECORD
set by Gary Mcdonald,
California
4.5 sec.

_____
MY TIME

Going beyond "This Little Piggy"

A Back Rub Story

This is a combination story/back rub. It's like "This Little Piggy Goes to Market" only it's for backs, not toes. You'll need a friend. Make them turn their back to you. As you tell the story, tap, brush, bump, scratch and tickle their back to go with the words.

This is what you read   This is what you do

There was a little girl who lived in a charming house (outline a house). Her Uncle Simon gave her a very special seed (make a dot for a seed) and told her how to plant it.

So the little girl took the seed, found a perfect spot and dug (pat pat pat) a hole in the ground. Then she dropped the seed into the hole and covered the hole with dirt (pat pat pat). She watered the seed (make little drops of rain) and left the seed in the hot sun (outline and pat the hot sun).

That night, it began to rain and rain (make rain dots). But eventually, the sun came out (outline the sun and pat pat pat) and the little seed began to grow (make seed grow 5 inches).

The next week there was a thunderstorm and lightning (make fist pats and quick firm pat pat pat) until finally the storm went away and the sun came out (draw sun circle and pat pat pat) and the little seed grew and grew and grew, all the way up your back (make the seed grow up to their neck).

And it was a beautiful flower.

The Universal Book Report

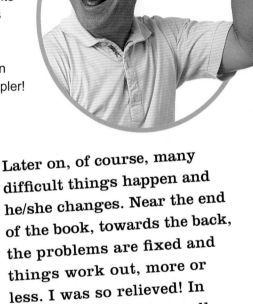

Sometimes, in our busy lives, we occasionally get stuck having to write a book report about a book whose details we don't entirely remember. That used to be a problem. Now, all you have to do is copy *The Universal Book Report* and fill in the blanks where it says! Life just got simpler!

After reading [BOOK TITLE] by [AUTHOR'S NAME] I am full of thoughts. Never before have I thought the thoughts that I am now thinking. And the feelings I am feeling are surely a result of those thoughts.

The lead character in [BOOK TITLE] was, I truly believe, the most important person. At the beginning of the book, we don't know him/her very well.

Later on, of course, many difficult things happen and he/she changes. Near the end of the book, towards the back, the problems are fixed and things work out, more or less. I was so relieved! In conclusion, I think we all learned an important lesson! I know that I certainly did!

Thank you.

The End.

How to Predict Your Height

The following formula has been used by real scientists.

Measure your mother and father.

If you're a girl, subtract 5 inches from your father's height. If you're a boy, add 5 inches to your mother's height. Add the adjusted heights of your parents and divide by 2.

To that number, add 2 inches to determine the upper limit of your predicted height. Subtract 2 inches to determine the lower limit of your predicted height. Your final height has a 90% chance of falling within those two limits.

In fly-years

How Old Are You?

You are SO old!

Flies only live about a month. Let's say humans live 70 years. So one fly-year equals about 800 human years, if we round down.

So, how old are YOU in fly-years?

_____ **x 800 =** _____

Your age in years   Your age in fly-years

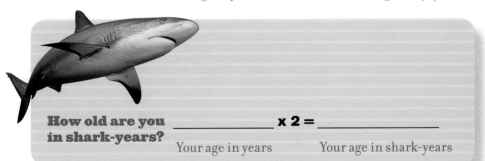

How old are you in shark-years? _____ **x 2 =** _____

Your age in years   Your age in shark-years

Betting on the ImpossiTables

☐ If you think these two tables are identical, check this box.

☐ If you think they aren't, check this one.

Cut out the "tablecloth" and use it to check yourself. If you got it right, and you weren't guessing, we're impressed. (We already know the answer, and we STILL get it wrong.)

Hang This Spoon from Your Nose

Cut this spoon out, get the back of it wet, and stick it to your nose. If you do that and let yourself be seen in public, know that you are a very immature person. We salute you.

But if you want to go even further, try the same idea with a real spoon.

Breathe on the bowl of a real spoon so it gets a little foggy (and so a little sticky). Lean your head way back, and press the bowl of the spoon on the bridge of your nose. Very slowly, bring your head down. Make sure other people are watching.

Cut out and hang from nose.

WANNA CHALLENGE?
We know a girl who can hang four spoons. Cheeks, nose, and chin.

Cell phone camera shots

Dude! You Dropped Your Head!

If you're one of those people who always look a little heavier in photographs, here's the perfect shot for you. Guaranteed to make you look 20 pounds lighter!

Get an
Insta-Do

How
we
did it

You Have Lost Your Last Coin Toss

Cut out this handy quarter cover, glue it to the tail side of any quarter, and the next time you're in a coin toss, just remember to say "Heads!"

Personal testimonial: We fixed up one of our own quarters like this and haven't lost a toss in years.
It's *amazing!*

How it should look:

Front

Back

Quarter Cover

Cut here.
Tape or glue to backside of quarter.

Brain candy

Why Is This Man Drinking Dinosaur Urine?

Because it's cool and refreshing, especially with ice. Of course, he doesn't KNOW it's dino pee; he thinks it's just water. And he's right. But what he doesn't realize is that water is old stuff. Really old.

Over the millions of years of its existence the H_2O molecules of water he is now drinking have been in every ocean, in every sea, and through many, many other bodies besides his.

What's all this mean for you? Simple. The next time you drink anything (water is the main ingredient in every liquid you'll ever drink), close your eyes and imagine a *T. rex* looking around for some prehistoric hydrant.

Cheers!

How to Make an Air Puff Annoyer

Rubber band

Balloon

With nothing more than a scrap of old balloon and a cardboard tube, you can launch invisible air rings and irritate people clear across the room.

Oatmeal box

Cut a 1-inch hole.

The hardest part is finding a big tube. Toilet paper tubes don't work. Cardboard oatmeal containers are perfect, but you can probably find something big and round around the house that has one end open and one end closed. Cut a hole in the center of the closed end and cover the open end like a drum (a piece of old balloon works fine, held in place by a rubber band).

Pull back and pop the rubber balloon like a drum skin and you'll be amazed how far you can launch little puffs of air — 10 feet is no problem if your cardboard tube is big enough.

10 feet

Snap the drum skin.

SCIENCE FAIR COMING UP? Some hardware stores sell short pieces of heating duct you could modify to make an air puff cannon, good for 20–30 feet!

Cut this name tag out and tape it to your forehead. That way, you'll finally get the respect you deserve. If a teacher demands a homework assignment from you, just slap this sticker on and say "Excuse me? Do you know who you're talking to?"

It's scientifically true, of course, because the universe is unbounded and thus every point within it has an equal claim to being the exact center.

Your claim just happens to be a little more equal than the others.

How
Floa

1. Hold knees tightly together.

2. Stick hands in between them.

3. Strain and strain. Try to separate your knees, but keep them locked for 60 seconds.

4. After 60 seconds release, close eyes, smile and float away.

Find Your Blind Spot

Hold this page at arm's length with your right hand. Close your left eye and look at the . You'll see the out of the corner of your eye. As you look at the , slowly bring the page towards your face. Notice when the disappears. Make the reappear by continuing to bring the card towards your face.

The disappears at the point where its image on your retina is exactly on the blind spot, the place where the optic nerve leaves the retina and goes to the brain. You are blind to any image that falls on this spot. You aren't normally aware of your blind spots because your eyes are always moving around. The brain fills in the information that is missing in the blind spot, a tiny area in your field of vision.

The Stepped-On Bubblegum Scale

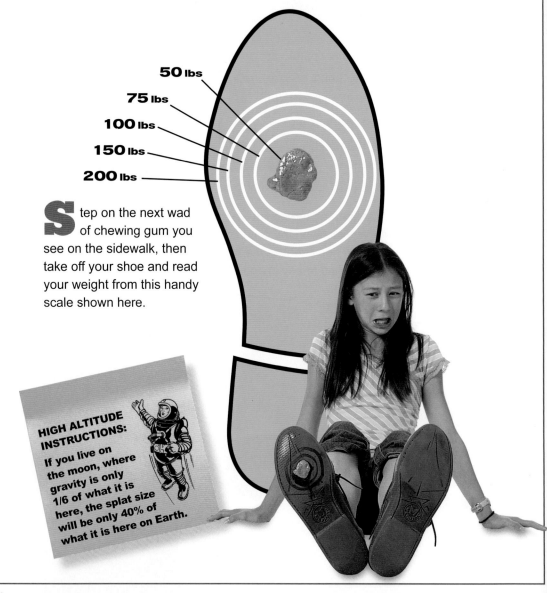

50 lbs
75 lbs
100 lbs
150 lbs
200 lbs

Step on the next wad of chewing gum you see on the sidewalk, then take off your shoe and read your weight from this handy scale shown here.

HIGH ALTITUDE INSTRUCTIONS:

If you live on the moon, where gravity is only 1/6 of what it is here, the splat size will be only 40% of what it is here on Earth.

Give Your Dog a Yawn

1 Stand in front of your dog and open your mouth really wide.

2 Leave it there for a while and make little gr~~ooning noises.~~

3 Re~~...~~
unt~~...~~

EXTRA CRED~~IT~~

We have given ~~...~~
and dogs many ~~...~~
our knowledge ~~...~~
recorded histo~~ry has ever g...~~
yawn to any other species. Many
leading yawn scientists believe
it is impossibl~~e...~~
disagree, and w~~...~~
public for help. If ~~...~~
yawn to any of the ~~...~~
species, please send us a
photo, or at least swear to
it in an e-mail. Science
needs your help!

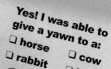

Yes! I was able to
give a yawn to a:
- ❑ horse
- ❑ rabbit
- ❑ cow
- ❑ bug
- ❑ fish
- ❑ hamster
- ❑ lizard
- ❑ frog

Make a Chinese Fortune Sandwich

Cut these fortunes out and, whenever possible, put them in people's sandwiches.

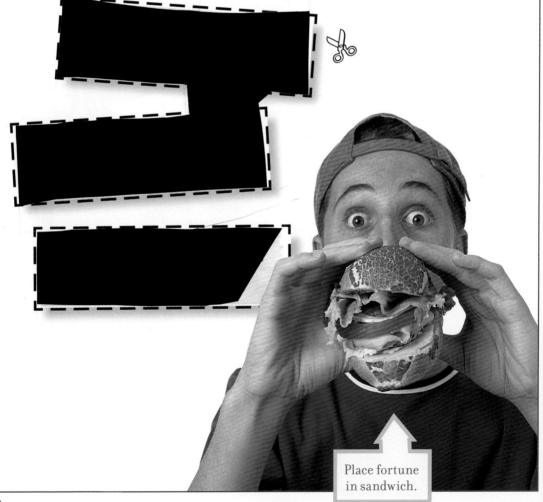

Place fortune in sandwich.

The Great American Ear Rub

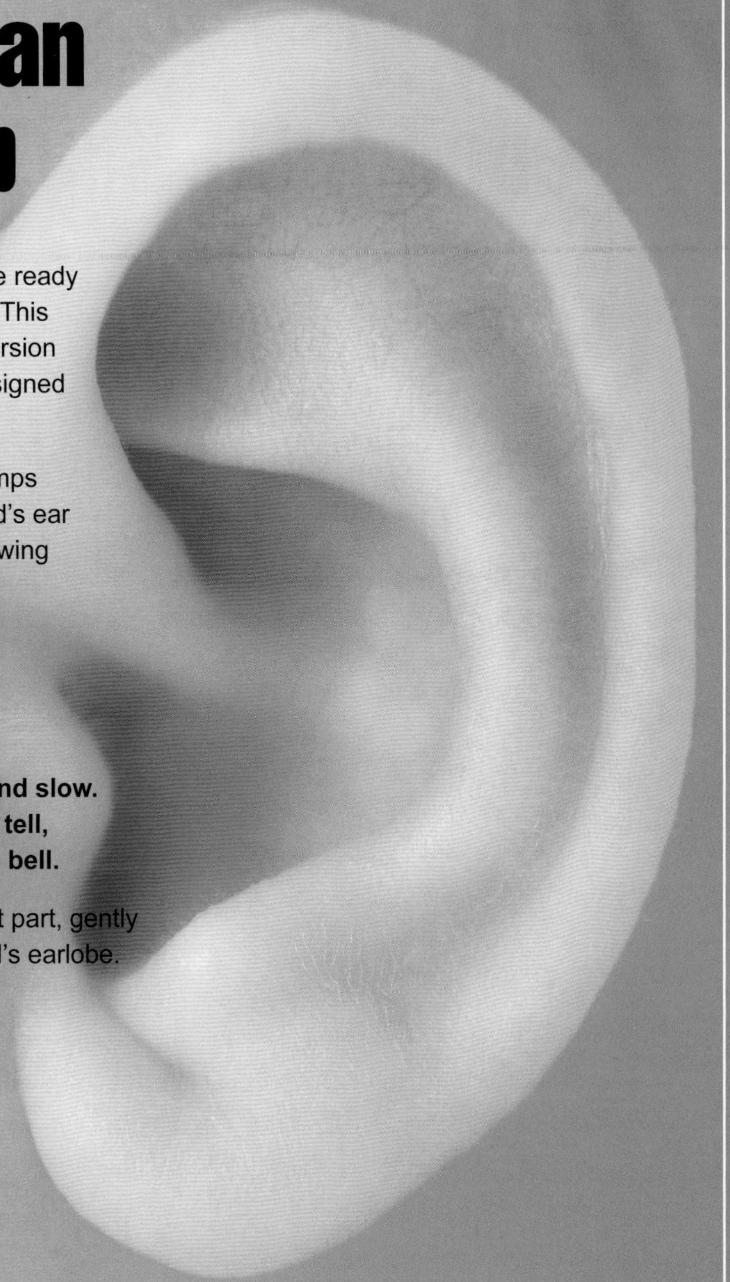

For people who are ready to move beyond "This Little Piggy," here is a version of the same idea but designed for ears, not toes.

Slowly rub the funny bumps and valleys of your friend's ear while you recite the following deathless poem.

**Round and round
and round and round
and round and round
the hills you go.
Drive the trolley nice and slow.
If it's safe and you can tell,
Don't forget to ring the bell.**

When you get to this last part, gently but firmly pull your friend's earlobe.

Ding Ding!

Can You Beat Gary Mcdonald in Pencil Athletics?

Gary Mcdonald is a friend of ours and is one of the country's leading pencil athletes.

He has completed the following events with **zero** penalty points, and he dropped a pencil right on the bull's-eye.

WINDING ROAD: Close eyes. Draw line from Ⓐ to Ⓑ without touching the fences. Every touch is a penalty point.

HURDLES: Close eyes. Draw line from Ⓐ to Ⓑ to Ⓒ… to Ⓘ without touching any hurdles. Every touch is a penalty point.

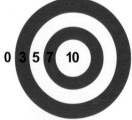

BULL'S-EYE: Close eyes. Drop pencil from 9 inches.

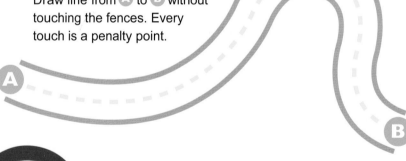

Are You Taking Good Care of Your Parasites?

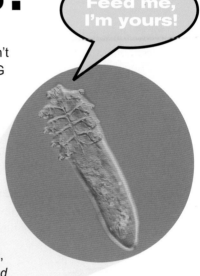

Feed me, I'm yours!

Are you one of those kids whose parents won't let them have pets because "Pets are a BIG responsibility!"?

Well, *guess what!* You're *already* taking good care of pets! Lots of them. They're the little bugs that live on your eyebrows and eyelashes — called *follicle mites*.

Sure they're small, but they need food, water and a warm place to sleep, just like cats and dogs! Tell your parents that you are the primary caregiver to all of your parasites, including your follicle mites, *and they are doing just fine, thank you very much!*

Here's a picture of a well-cared-for follicle mite. If you had a microscope, you could look at yours and give them names. About four would live comfortably on the period at the end of this sentence.

Backseat Rituals

Sitting in the backseat of a car does not come without responsibilities. Please read and observe the following rituals. They're ancient and they matter. Don't ask why.

Graveyards and Tunnels

Whenever you drive by a graveyard, you must hold your breath until you have passed it entirely. This rule also holds for all tunnels.

Punchbuggy

Whoever sees a Volkswagen® and is able to holler "Punchbuggy" first, gets to punch his seatmate in the shoulder.

Hay Wagon Wishes

If you see a truck filled with hay, and you make a wish, and you don't see the truck again, your wish will come true.

Padiddle

If you are the first to see a car with only one headlight working, you holler **"Padiddle!"** and kiss the person next to you. For the squeamish, you can touch the roof instead.

Trucker Honk

If you see a big truck, the 18-wheeler kind, look hopefully at the driver and pump your arm up and down, as if you were pulling a steam whistle on an old train. The friendlier drivers will honk for you.

River Crossings

Whenever you cross a bridge, you must lift your feet (so they don't get wet).

Cow Alert

If you are the first to spot a cow, you get to holler "Cow Alert!" and everyone else holds their noses and says "Peeee Euuuuuw!"

Can You Tongue-Punch This Paper?

Punch here.

Hold this paper up tightly to your face, take a deep breath and tightly coil your tongue. Then, suddenly, with whip-like force, lash out and see if you can tongue-punch a hole in this paper.

Newspaper will withstand 10 pounds per square inch of force. If you can punch this paper (we couldn't), that is the equivalent of a 460-pound bench press.

Tomorrow's championship round? Cardboard!

How to Shake Ankles

1 Approach as if for normal handshake.

2 Reach for hand... but miss to the outside.

3 Lean over, grab their ankle and shake vigorously. So that they may do the same, lift your own ankle up simultaneously.

Another back rub story

X Marks the Spot

Back rub stories are stories that you tell while you're tapping, thumping, squeezing, pinching and rubbing your friend's back.
Here's another one.

This is what you read
This is what you do

X marks the spot (draw a big X in the middle of his back) With a circle (draw a circle) And a dot (poke your finger into the middle of the circle) Spider's going down (run your fingers down his back) Spider's going up (run your fingers up his back) Owww! You got a bite! (squeeze the back of his neck)

Blooooooood rushing down (run your fingers down) Blooooooood rushing down (do it again) Squeeze some oranges on your shoulders (squeeze both his shoulders) Let the juice drip down (run your fingers down his back) Let the juice drip down (run your fingers down his back) Now guess the magic letter (draw a letter on his back) Or I won't go on (he has to guess it before you go on)

Needles in your neck (drum your fingers on the back of his neck) And a knife in your back (thump him lightly in the back) Means the bloooood drips down (run your fingers down his back) Means the bloooood drips down (run your fingers down his back) Needles in your neck (drum your fingers on the back of his neck) And a knife in your back (thump him lightly in the back) Means the bloooood drips down (run your fingers down his back) Means the bloooood drips down (run your fingers down his back) Feel the cool breeze (blow gently on the back of his neck) Then a tight squeeze (squeeze the back of his neck lightly) Now you've got the shiveries.

Try the World's Hardest 3-Piece Jigsaw Puzzle

Photocopy this page, then cut along dotted lines. End up with three pieces. Then put the riders on the horses. Simple? Try it.

End up with these three pieces.

Answer in back.

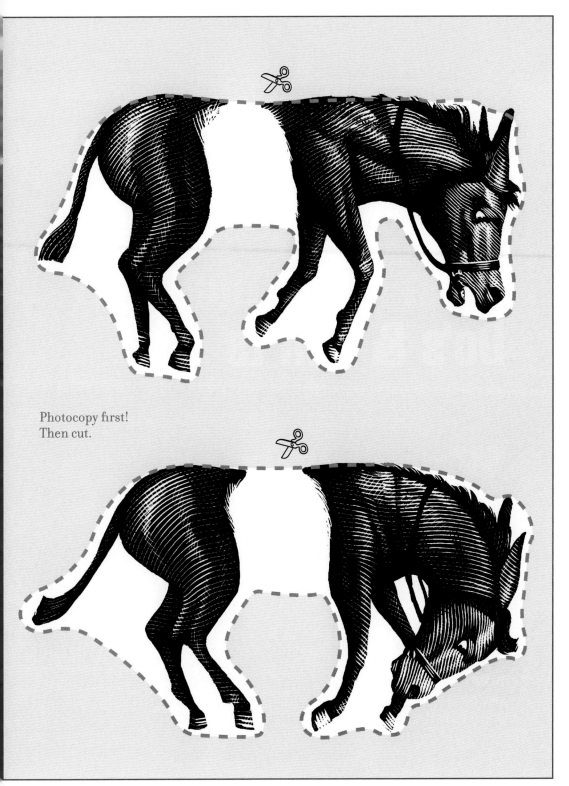

Photocopy first!
Then cut.

Alien Abduction
Do's & Don'ts

Would you know what to do if YOU were abducted by aliens? A surprising number of kids do not. That's why we are publishing this page for you to cut out. Keep it handy, because you… just… never… know.

DO identify which are the aliens, and which are furniture.

DO comply with all alien instructions, even if you don't understand them.

DO ask to use the restroom before leaving the command center.

DON'T try to drive the spaceship, take pictures, chew with your mouth open or use "The Force."

Walk This Through Door

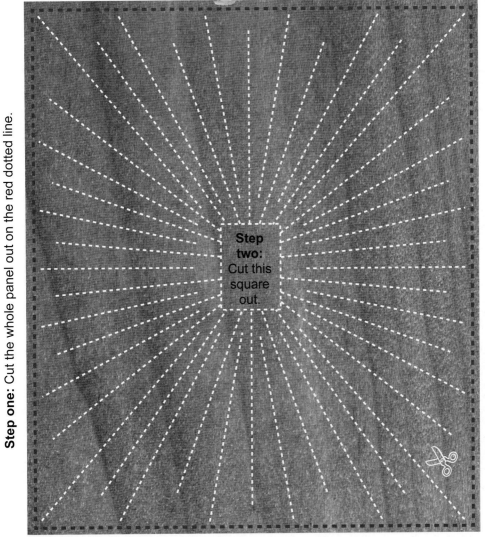

Step one: Cut the whole panel out on the red dotted line.

Step two: Cut this square out.

Step three: Cut exactly on the dotted white lines.

If you are good with scissors and can stay on the dotted lines, you can turn this panel into a paper doughnut big enough to walk through (true story).

Who yelled, "Coming are the British."?
Paul Reverse.

What do the letters D N A stand for?
National Dyslexics' Association.

What do Eskimos get from sitting on the ice too long?
Polaroids.

Why do golfers wear two pairs of pants?

In case they get a hole in one.

What do you get when you pour boiling water down a rabbit hole?
Hot cross bunnies.

Why did the bunnies go on strike?
They wanted a raise in celery.

How do you make an elephant fly?
First, you start with a 48-inch zipper...

Do you know why gorillas have such big nostrils?
Have you ever seen their fingers?

If at first you don't succeed, do not try skydiving.

A man is talking to a psychiatrist and says: "I'm feeling suicidal, Doc. What do you recommend?"
The doctor says: "Pay in advance."

Break Down Your Brain

We took an X-ray and discovered the contents of our dog's brain. Here it is. You might like to know how your own brain breaks down. If so, here is a pie chart for you to fill in by connecting the dots. Afterwards, cut it out and put it on the fridge so others may know you better.

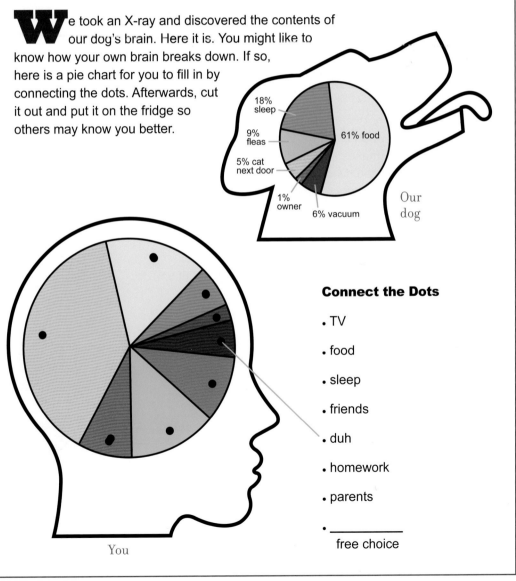

18% sleep

9% fleas

5% cat next door

1% owner

6% vacuum

61% food

Our dog

You

Connect the Dots

- TV
- food
- sleep
- friends
- duh
- homework
- parents
- _____ free choice

Write a "first-time sentence"

"Your Brain Smells Like Moon Pie Dumplings"

The Challenge: Construct a sentence that makes some kind of sense, but that NO ONE, in the history of history, has ever ever said or written before. When you think you've done it, fill in the blank below.

Extra credit Use a marker and write your sentence on the bottom of a flip-flop. Then mail to us with no package. See pages 2 and 223. If you do, we will send you our *You Are an Amazing Person* certificate.

Fill in the blanks

The sentence below has never been written or said before in the English language. You read it here first.

_____

_____

_____

_____

Department of Dodged Bullets

What's Your "Almost Name"?

What do you think life would have been like if you had been named something like Casper? Or Erma? Pretty scary, huh?

Well, guess what! Real-life parents actually consider these kinds of names when they are getting ready to name their babies! It's true! Ask your own parents what your "almost name" was. You won't believe how close you came to a life of shame and embarrassment.

P.S. A former governor of Texas, James Hogg, actually did name his little girl Ima.

HELLO
My Almost Name Is

A quick reference
Homework Excuses

Sometimes, you just can't remember why it is you didn't do your homework last night. If that's your problem, here's your answer.

I sprained my brain. The doctor says no heavy thinking for a week.

I have a rare paper allergy.

Why should I do homework when the universe is winding down and the sun will explode in 50 billion years?

I already finished school in a previous lifetime. I'm only going now for the lunches.

Excuse me? I don't speak English. But thank you for asking. One day I hope to learn your language. In the meantime, I'm just faking it.

I finished my homework in my head. Why write it down and waste a tree?

My horoscope said, "Avoid homework or you will turn into a frog." Can you believe it, Mom? A frog! Whew!… We dodged a bullet.

Didn't you hear about the kid who got TOO smart? He made his mom and dad feel dumb. I would never do that to my parents.

I have decided to submit last night's homework to a major broadcaster for a television sitcom pilot. In the meantime, my agent tells me that I can't show it to anyone else.

How to Set the Table in Australia

Do you ever get tired of seeing glasses filled with water on a table, especially when they're all right-side up? How boring is that! Follow these simple diagrams and you'll learn how they do it in Australia — upside-down style.

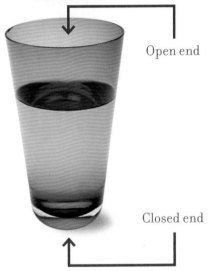

Open end

Closed end

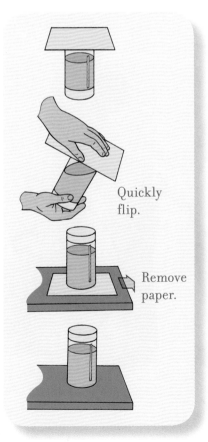

Quickly flip.

Remove paper.

Follow these directions

1. Cover a half-filled plastic glass with a (thick) piece of paper. Manila folder is good.

2. Hold it in place and quickly flip the cup upside down and set it on the table. Speed matters.

3. Slowly, carefully, remove the paper. Done!

For directions on how to get the cup off the table without making a mess and really irritating your mother, call: 1-800-IMIN TROUBLENOW!

Or at least fake it

How to Tear Off Your Friend's Belt Loop

Catch the tip of your finger like this and…

How many times have you stood in line behind somebody and gotten really irritated by their belt loop? And you didn't know what to do about it? Well, here's an easy suggestion — rip it off!

Imagine that you're standing behind your friend in line. Suddenly, he feels you grab his belt loop, tug on it, and the sound of ripping fabric is clearly heard. Won't he be surprised!

Actually, it's a trick. Look at the photographs for the technique.

Key Point:
Don't pull <u>straight</u> back. You'll tear off the loop.

You'll make a snapping noise if you slip your finger to the side as you pull.

Random, or are they aiming?

Why Do Birds Poop on YOUR Head?

Bingo!

Have you ever sat down and thought much about the mathematics of bird poop? Why, for example, have YOU taken so many head shots? Random? Just your luck?

That's what WE used to think too. But then we did the math... 300 million heads in the U.S. x 50 square inches/head = 2,500 acres of head or .0001% of the country's acreage. Work that out (a billion birds, 10 poops/day), and if it were strictly random, we should each of us get hit no more than once every 5 years. Yeah, right. How does that jibe with YOUR experience?

WAKE UP PEOPLE! We are bird toilets! They laugh at us in their nests! They tally up hits!!

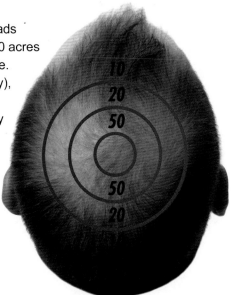

10
20
50

50
20

Bird's-eye view

Do you have a problem with insect nudity?

Cut-Out Clothes for Your Bugs

Are the bugs around your house and yard naked? Is that a problem for you? If so, we have your solution right here: fashion-forward, ready-to-wear paper outfits designed to be worn by bugs that you can cut out and paste on. *Note about sizes:* These bug outfits are XXXXXS, pretty average for a bug. If your bugs are larger or smaller, just use a photocopy machine to make the adjustments.

Fly Cape

Beetle Sportcoat

Snail Stickers

Hey! Watch Your Step!

How Am I Sliming? 1-800-SLOMO

Take control of your future

How to Write Palms

Don't let your future be controlled by the lines on your hand. At least not the ones that are already there. Re-write your hand and take back your life!

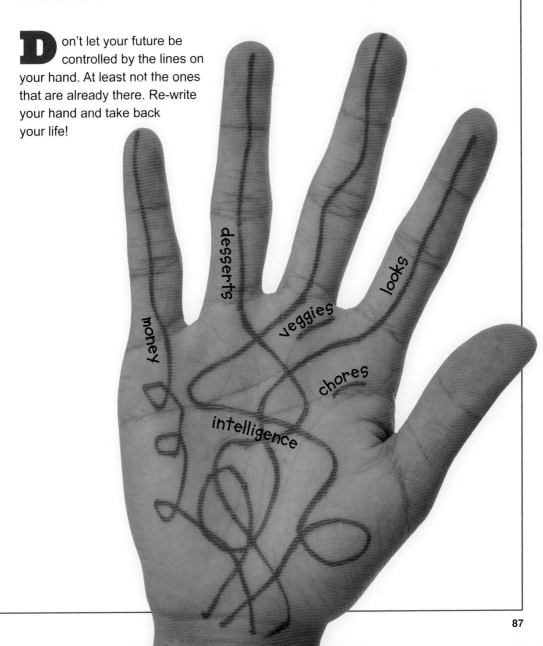

money

desserts

veggies

looks

chores

intelligence

The In-Mouth Cherry Stem Knot Challenge

According to leading scientists, only 18 people in North America are fully capable of putting a cherry stem into their mouths and tying it into a knot with tongue power alone!

Are you one of these remarkable people? We would be happy to include instructions, but we can't do it ourselves. Sorry. You're on your own. We think you have to use your teeth, though.

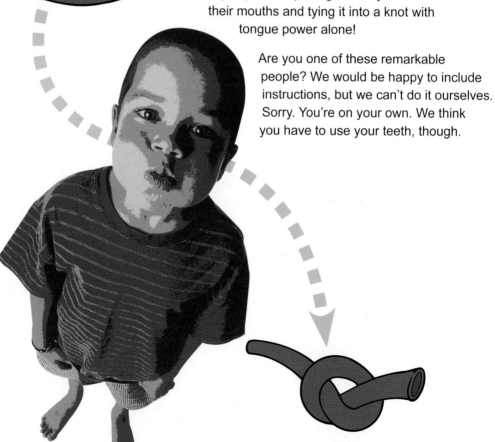

Dumb Joke Wallet Cards

Cut out. Cover with clear tape. Insert in wallet.

QUICK REFERENCE CARD No. 1

Q: If a cannibal ate his mother's sister, what would you call him?
A: An aunt-eater.

I have a very frustrated pet at home. It's a turtle that loves to chase cars.

Hello, operator? I'd like to speak to the king of the jungle. Sorry, sir, but the lion is busy right now.

Q: Where do astronauts leave their spaceships?
A: At parking meteors.

AWFUL FOR ANY OCCASION

QUICK REFERENCE CARD No. 2

Q: What's green, salty and giggles?
A: A dill tickle.

Q: What do you call a clairvoyant short person who just broke out of prison?
A: A small medium at large.

Q: How do you keep a skunk from smelling?
A: Hold its nose.

Q: What kind of shoes do you make out of banana peels?
A: Slippers.

You: How can you keep a fool in suspense?
Your friend: How?
You:

AWFUL FOR ANY OCCASION

QUICK REFERENCE CARD No. 3

A couple of fleas were leaving a theatre. One asked the other, "You want to fly home or take a dog?"

Q: Why do bees hum?
A: They can never remember the words.

Q: What do you get if you cross a lake with a leaky boat?
A: About half way.

Q: Where does the Lone Ranger take his garbage?
A: To the dump, to the dump, to the dump, dump, dump.

AWFUL FOR ANY OCCASION

QUICK REFERENCE CARD No. 4

Q: What do you call a rabbit with a lot of fleas?
A: Bugs Bunny.

Teacher: What time is it?
Student: Right now?

Q: What lies on the ground a hundred feet in the air?
A: A dead centipede.

Q: What has four wheels and flies?
A: A garbage truck.

Q: What was the last thing to enter the bug's mind as he hit the windshield?
A: His back legs.

AWFUL FOR ANY OCCASION

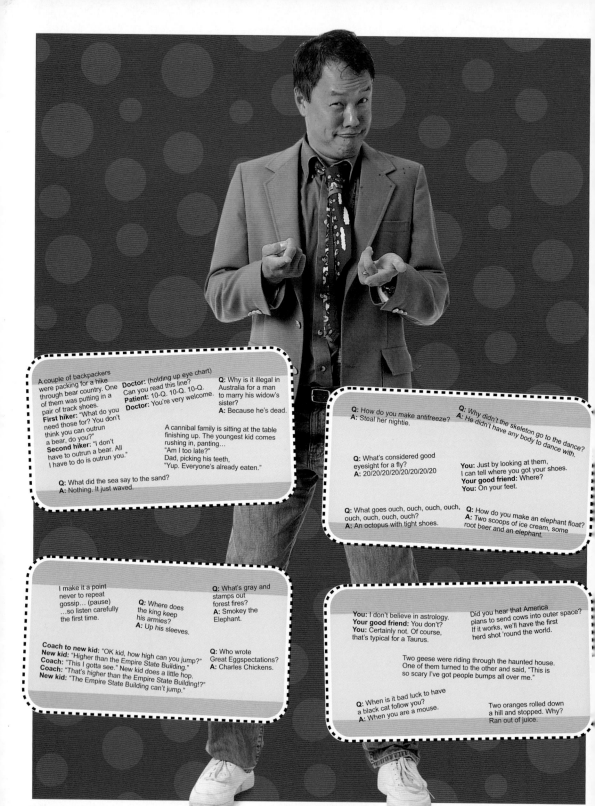

A couple of backpackers were packing for a hike through bear country. One of them was putting in a pair of track shoes.
First hiker: "What do you need those for? You don't think you can outrun a bear, do you?"
Second hiker: "I don't have to outrun a bear. All I have to do is outrun you."

Q: What did the sea say to the sand?
A: Nothing. It just waved.

Doctor: (holding up eye chart) Can you read this line?
Patient: 10-Q. 10-Q. 10-Q.
Doctor: You're very welcome.

A cannibal family is sitting at the table finishing up. The youngest kid comes rushing in, panting…
"Am I too late?"
Dad, picking his teeth,
"Yup. Everyone's already eaten."

Q: Why is it illegal in Australia for a man to marry his widow's sister?
A: Because he's dead.

Q: How do you make antifreeze?
A: Steal her nightie.

Q: Why didn't the skeleton go to the dance?
A: He didn't have any body to dance with.

Q: What's considered good eyesight for a fly?
A: 20/20/20/20/20/20/20/20

You: Just by looking at them, I can tell where you got your shoes.
Your good friend: Where?
You: On your feet.

Q: What goes ouch, ouch, ouch, ouch, ouch, ouch, ouch, ouch?
A: An octopus with tight shoes.

Q: How do you make an elephant float?
A: Two scoops of ice cream, some root beer and an elephant.

I make it a point never to repeat gossip… (pause) …so listen carefully the first time.

Q: Where does the king keep his armies?
A: Up his sleeves.

Q: What's gray and stamps out forest fires?
A: Smokey the Elephant.

Coach to new kid: "OK kid, how high can you jump?"
New kid: "Higher than the Empire State Building."
Coach: "This I gotta see." New kid does a little hop.
Coach: "That's higher than the Empire State Building!?"
New kid: "The Empire State Building can't jump."

Q: Who wrote Great Eggspectations?
A: Charles Chickens.

You: I don't believe in astrology.
Your good friend: You don't?
You: Certainly not. Of course, that's typical for a Taurus.

Did you hear that America plans to send cows into outer space? If it works, we'll have the first herd shot 'round the world.

Two geese were riding through the haunted house. One of them turned to the other and said, "This is so scary I've got people bumps all over me."

Q: When is it bad luck to have a black cat follow you?
A: When you are a mouse.

Two oranges rolled down a hill and stopped. Why? Ran out of juice.

90

Quick reference excuses

The Case Against Chores

Alot of kids know they don't want to do chores, but they can't always remember why it's not fair that they have to do them. To solve that problem, here are a few handy arguments:

"Let's not clean. Let's move!"

"Mom, seriously. Our time together is so short. Let's not waste it 'cleaning.'"

"'Cleanliness' is NOT next to 'Godliness.' It's next to 'clay.' I looked it up."

"My room isn't a mess, it's a personal expression. It took me a long time to make it like this. If I were to change it in any way *(lower voice)*, I would be untrue to myself, AND *(sniff, sniff)* my art."

On your former friend's arm

How to Draw a Mouse

Ask a friend to trust you for a moment. You're going to show them how to draw a cute little mouse on their hand.

Here's how it goes:

"...and then, you need a... **tail!!**"

"First, you draw a little tiny nose."

"Then, a pair of cute little eyes..."

1 Draw a little dot.

2 Draw two more little dots.

3 Draw a big line up the arm. And run.

Captain Klutz
Decoder Badges

Cut these badges out and assemble them to join our exclusive **Klutz Sneaky Club.**

Cut the small wheel out. Center it on the larger wheel and join with a brad.

Line up the **J** to the **q**. So now the **C** lines up to the **j**; the **A** lines up to the **h**; and the **T** lines up to the **a**.

So **CAT** is now spelled **jha**. **DOG** is spelled **kvn**.

You can use these decoder badges to send notes to a sneaky friend, or you can use them to answer the following questions.

All the toilet seats were stolen from police headquarters. Now the police have nothing **av nv vu**.

Q: Where do you find a no-legged dog?

A: ypnoa dolyl fvb slma opt

Q: What do the letters DNA stand for?

A: uhapvuhs kfzslepj hzzvjphapvu

Q: How much do pirates pay for their earrings?

A: h ibjjhully

Answers in back.

Cut everything out! Punch out the middles and use a brad to put the circles together. Join the little circles to the big circles.

KEEP THIS WHEEL!
Future secret messages will need it!

DECODER WHEEL

94

Physics gets phun!

The Home Tennis Ball Launcher!

ou'll need a basketball and a tennis ball. Stack them as shown.

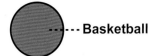 ····· **Tennis ball**

····· **Basketball**

Then drop the stack onto the ground, making sure you're out of the way. The tennis ball will shoot straight up and the basketball will stop dead.

Try this:
For even more impressive results try the same thing with a Ping-Pong® ball instead of a tennis ball.

The world's finest paper airplane
The Nakamura Lock

On October 5, 1997, in a very light wind, we flew a Nakamura Lock from the press box at Stanford Football Stadium to the scoreboard. That's about 75 yards, with no loss of altitude. Took almost a minute to get there. If it hadn't hit the scoreboard, it would have been out of the stadium and would probably still be flying. Our opinion? Finest plane on the planet for performance and simplicity of fold.

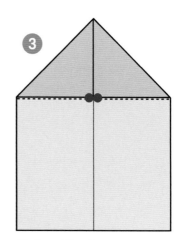

1 Begin by folding an 8½ x 11 sheet of paper in half the long way. Crease firmly, then unfold.

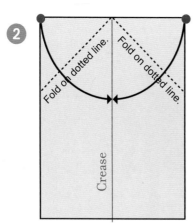

2 Fold on dotted line. Fold on dotted line. Crease

Fold corners (red dots) to the middle. Be really precise.

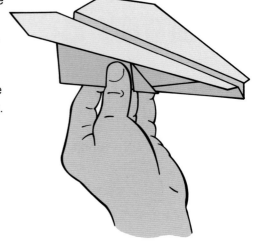

3

End up like this.

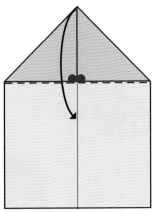

4 Fold on dotted line.

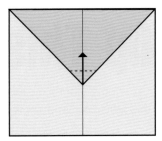

5 End up like this. Then put a crease on the red dotted line.

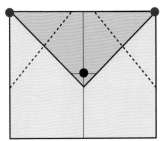

6 Fold top corners (red dots) into the middle where the purple dot is.

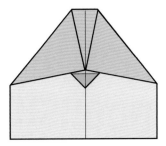

7 Find the center tip (we colored it green). Get ready to fold it…

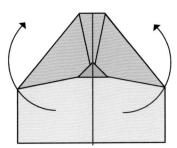

8 …up. Then fold the entire plane in half along the red line.

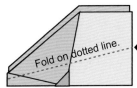

Fold on dotted line.

9 On each side, fold the wings down. Be crisp and precise.

Last fold is critical. Do it at the **exact** mid-point. Mark it with a pencil if you want.

Finished folding.

News you can use

Clip This Article

Tear this article out and show it to your parents.

Supreme Court Rules Homework Unconstitutional

9-0 Unanimous Vote

WASHINGTON — The Supreme Court handed down a historic decision today in a case that has been closely watched by educators and students alike. The issue was the constitutionality of homework. The specific case (Wilbur B. Everykid v. U.S. Board of Education) pitted Everykid, who acted as his own lawyer, against a team of highly trained professional government attorneys.

"When truth and justice are on your side," said Everykid, "who needs a fancy degree?"

The justices ruled that homework violates the 8th amendment ("cruel and unusual punishment"), the 9th amendment ("government intrusion") and the 18th amendment guaranteeing "television without distraction."

The new ruling takes effect immediately and renders all outstanding assignments null and void. As for past homework, teachers will be expected to compensate students by paying them "a meaningful amount."

Making a Soda Gusher

If you want to be unscientific about it, carbonated soda is like an overcrowded prison. All that carbon dioxide gas has been forced into the water and now it's trapped inside, rattling on its bars, desperate to get out.

Ordinarily when you open a bottle and drink it, the prisoners get out one by one — bubble by bubble — organized but not very exciting. However, it IS possible to engineer a jailbreak — a gassy riot where they all rush the gates and gusher out at once. That's a lot more fun. Here's how to do it:

1. **Buy a package of Mentos® mints.** Or, if you can't be bothered, use plain old salt. The gusher is still pretty good, just not quite as tall.

2. **Buy a 2-liter bottle of diet soda pop.** The diet makes a slightly better gusher, plus it's easier to clean up, if you care about that kind of thing.

3. **Make a paper tube and put it over the opened bottle.** Pinch bottom, fill the tube with a stack of Mentos, place over opened bottle… and release! Stand WAY back.

Mentos go in here.

Pinch at the X to hold the Mentos. Let go when it's time.

And other duct stuff

Make Duct Tape Underpants

Are you tired of paying high prices for your duct tape undergarments? Here is a photo to help you make your own. Right next to a photo of a fork made out of duct tape, for those occasions when your hosts come up one fork short.

Additional inspiration: Duct tape visionaries abound on the Web, where you can easily find prom dresses, wallets, purses, etc.

Fork

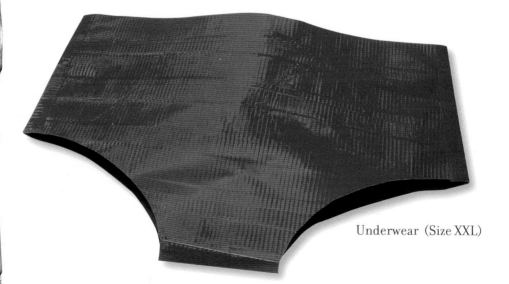

Underwear (Size XXL)

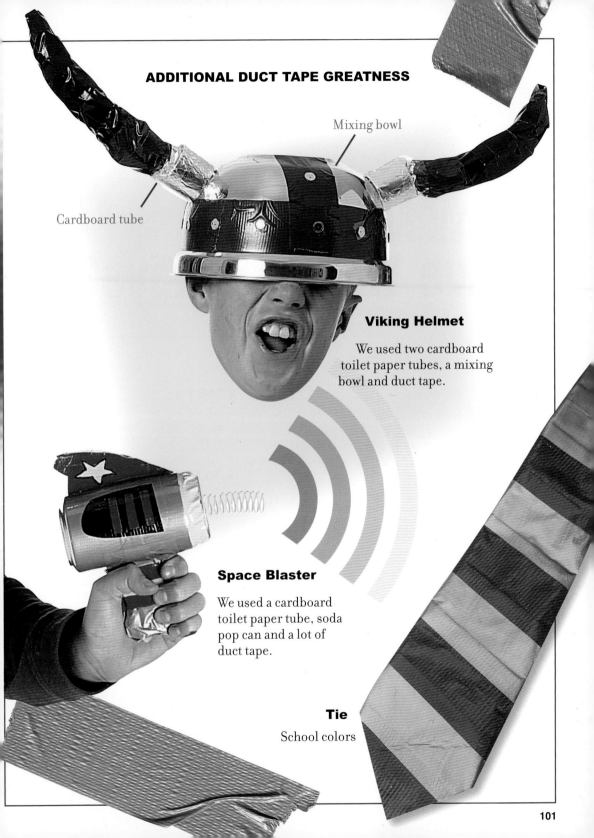

ADDITIONAL DUCT TAPE GREATNESS

Mixing bowl

Cardboard tube

Viking Helmet

We used two cardboard toilet paper tubes, a mixing bowl and duct tape.

Space Blaster

We used a cardboard toilet paper tube, soda pop can and a lot of duct tape.

Tie

School colors

Wanna feel old?

How Many Days Have You Been Alive?

1

_____ **x 365 =** _____

How old I am

2

_____ **x 30.5 =** _____

Number of months
since last birthday

3 Today's date is the _____ .

Do all three of these math problems.
Then add all the answers together.

_____ + _____ + _____ = _____

    1   2   3

Number of days
I've been alive

Are You Getting All the Birthdays You Deserve?

Back in the old days, kids only got presents and stuff every 365 days. Today, though, we live in a metric digital era, and leading scientists recommend that kids get birthdays every 100 days, and really special birthdays every 1,000 days.

Of course none of this is meant to replace the traditional system. It's just an addition.

These are your **METRIC** birthdays.
Mark your calendar.

- **When you are 2 years, 8 months, 27 days you are 1,000 days old.**
- **When you are 5 years, 5 months, 23 days you are 2,000 days old.**
- **When you are 8 years, 2 months, 19 days you are 3,000 days old.**
- **When you are 10 years, 11 months, 14 days you are 4,000 days old.**
- **When you are 13 years, 8 months, 9 days you are 5,000 days old.**

How Many People in the World Look Exactly Like You?

You have a secret twin out there in the world somewhere. Actually, you have about 40. How do we know?

Simple. We used the scientifically unproven Elvis Impersonator Theory. Out of the 4,000 or so professional Elvis impersonators, only about 1% actually look like him. Therefore, it follows with strict logic that there must be a similar number out there who could impersonate you (maybe they wouldn't make quite as much money at it, but still...).

What this means is very simple. Forty people are out there with only one face: yours.

Scary.

Storage for Pre-Chewed Gum

Don't you hate it when you stick your old gum somewhere, like under your desk, and then, when you come back, it's gone! Stolen!

Klutz to the rescue! Just punch out these handy storage units and stick your gum onto them when you need to rest it. Indicate date and how much flavor is left.

Stay Away! This is MY gum!
(stick gum here)
Date?_____ Flavor left?_____%

Stay Away! This is MY gum!
(stick gum here)
Date?_____ Flavor left?_____%

Stay Away! This is MY gum!
(stick gum here)
Date?_____ Flavor left?_____%

Stay Away! This is MY gum!
(stick gum here)
Date?_____ Flavor left?_____%

How to Get Free Stuff in the Mail

The President
ACME Ice Cream Co.
450 Lambert Ave.
Palo Alto, CA 94306

ME

The next time the dog chews up one of your toys, or you drop an ice cream cone, or a book gets wet in the rain, try mailing a nice note to the company that made whatever it was you just lost. It might be a waste of time, or you might get lucky and get something back!

Big tip: Follow the example above exactly! Draw a picture of yourself on the envelope in crayon. Write the note by hand and go straight to the top — address it to the President and use the address on the package.

Make a Marshmallow Blowgun

Get a file folder, a piece of tape and a marshmallow.

Roll the folder into a marshmallow-size tube and tape it shut.

Insert marshmallow.

Blow. If you want more power, rub your marshmallows in flour first. They won't stick so much.

If you have a friend or younger siblings nearby, you should invent fun games to play, like "Stand There and Be a Human Target."

Roll from corner to corner.

How to Play the Telephone

Next time you're on the phone to a friend, and they question your musical talent, play them a tune! Hit the buttons as shown.

America
5 5 6 1 5 9
My coun- try, 'tis of thee,
0 0 8 0 8 4
sweet land of li- ber- ty,
8 4 2 4
of thee I sing

London Bridge
9 # 9 6 3 6 9
Lon- don Bridge is fall- ing down,
2 3 6 3 6 9
fall- ing down, fall- ing down.
9 # 9 6 3 6 9
Lond- on Bridge is fall- ing down,
2 9 3 1
my fair la- dy.

Twinkle, Twinkle, Little Star
1 1 9 9 0 0 9
Twin- kle, twin- kle, lit- tle star

Happy Birthday
4 4 2 4 # 8 1 1 2 1 9 8
Hap- py birth- day to you, hap- py birth- day to you

Hit yourself in the head

Make a Paper Boomerang

1 Cut on dotted lines.

2 Throw like this. Upright and spinning.

3 Duck.

Read This!

Actually, if you just cut your boomerang out of paper like we tell you to, it won't work. Sorry. It WILL work if you cut it out of cardboard or even manila file folder. Make it a little bigger, too.

Can STAND This ?

Can $\frac{\text{STAND}}{\text{U}}$ This ?

1 SAND	**2** $\frac{\text{MAN}}{\text{BOARD}}$	**3** $\frac{\text{STAND}}{\text{I}}$	**4** |R|E|A|D|I|N|G|
5 $\frac{\text{WEAR}}{\text{LONG}}$	**6** R ROA D A D	**7** T O W N	**8** CYCLE CYCLE CYCLE
9 LE VEL	**10** $\frac{0}{\text{M.D.}}$ Ph.D. B.S.	**11** $\frac{\text{KNEE}}{\text{LIGHTS}}$	**12** II ooo oo
13 CHAIR	**14** DICE DICE	**15** T O U C H	**16** GROUND FEET FEET FEET FEET FEET FEET
17 $\frac{\text{MIND}}{\text{MATTER}}$	**18** HE'S/HIMSELF	**19** ECNALG	**20** DEATH/LIFE
21 $\frac{\text{G.I.}}{\text{CCC}}$ CC C	**22** _ PROGRAM	**23** ⊢————⊣OME	**24** J U YOU S ME T

THE COLLEGE EXAM

The first one is "sandbox"; the second one is "man overboard"; the third one is…

CONNECT THE SQUARES

Draw a line connecting the two blue squares to each other. Draw another line connecting the two red squares to each other. Do the same for the green and the purple squares. One rule: The lines can't cross each other or go out of the box.

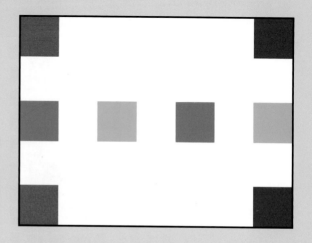

Answers in back.

Fridge Stickers

Does your mom try to make you eat rotten, dangerous, ancient food ("leftovers")? If so, try sticking these on the fridge. Tell her the health department put them up.

NO ENTRY

CODE RED

HAZMAT ALERT

"Excuse me, sir. Are you an attorney?"

"Yes."

"What is your fee?"

"A hundred dollars for every four questions."

"Isn't that terribly expensive?"

"Yes. What's your fourth question?"

What do you call a boomerang that doesn't work? A stick.

Why is abbreviation such a long word?

Horse walks into a bar. Bartender says, "So how come the long face?"

Why do they put bells on cows? Because their horns don't work.

Who was the idiot who put the letter s in "lisp"?

So the baby snake says to the mommy snake, "Hey, Mom, are we poisonous?"

Mommy snake says, "Why are you asking?"

Baby snake says: "Because I just bit my tongue."

My grandmother is in terrific shape. She started walking five miles a day when she was 60. She's 88 today, and we have no idea where she is.

Why don't cannibals eat comedians? They taste funny.

What's Your Official Klutz ID Number?

Whenever you correspond with us, please use your *Klutz ID Number* alongside your name. It allows us to keep our relationship with you and the rest of our readers as efficient, cold and impersonal as possible. **Thank you very much.**

Please answer the following questions:

_____ **Number of times you ordinarily sneeze at once?**

_____ **How much do you like green beans (score 1–10)?**

_____ **Last digit on your phone number?**

_____ **How old were you when you got out of diapers?**

_____ **Maximum number of pancakes you've eaten at one sitting?**

[Add the first four numbers and deduct the last.]

_____ **TOTAL**

If your number is:

<5 You are not doing the math right or you eat way too many pancakes.

5–20 You are a reasonable sneezer who understands green beans.

21–50 You are a vegetable with a phone.

51+ You are a serious sneezer who is still in diapers.

My Klutz ID number is

fill in your number

Make a fake pocket protector!

Would You Like to Be a Lot Smarter?

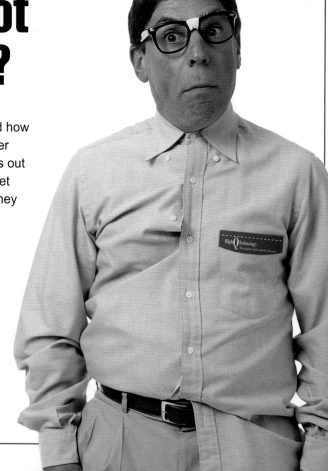

Have you ever wondered how come all those computer engineers are so smart? It turns out there's a secret! It's those pocket protectors they all wear! Sure they look dumb, but they actually enlarge your brain! Scientists don't understand why, but who cares? Anyway, here's yours. It's fake, but as long as it fools your brain, that's all that matters. Cut it out, put it on and you'll feel the effects immediately!

Light Switch Costumes

Are your light switches like ours? Are they white and square and do they just sort of sit there? Well, maybe it's time to give one of them a *Light Switch Makeover!* Cut along the dotted lines and tape them on.

 Cut and tape.

Cut and tape.

What is Y1K? The cause of the Dark Ages.

Duck walks into a drugstore and asks: "Do you sell lip balm?" Clerk says: "Yeah. But how are you going to pay for it?" "Oh, just put in on my bill."

Why did the toilet paper roll down the hill?

It wanted to get to the bottom.

Man goes to see his doctor. Doctor looks him over and says: "You've got ten to live." Man says "Ten what? Months? Years?" Doc: "10, 9, 8, 7..."

Termite goes into a bar and asks, "Is the bar tender here?"

Here's Your Re-Usable Dollar

Don't you hate it when the clerk takes your money at a store and then doesn't give it back? We sure do! That's why we invented *Re-Usable Money.* Here's how it works!

INSTRUCTIONS: Cut this bill out, cover it with clear tape on both sides to make it sturdier, then punch a hole in it and attach a few feet of string. Then, whenever you pay for something, and the guy takes your money and won't give it back — just hang on to the string and give it a quick jerk! Easy!

Name That Doodle!

The first answer:
Flies on a tightrope.

Use your decoder (see p.93) to find the other answers. (Code: c = S.)

1

2 czkqrodds cobfon li k fobi ybqkxsjon gksdob.

3 k pvi cdemu sx kx smo dbki.

5 k wyeco ryvo gsdr k nyyblovv.

4 k cxygwkx gsdr k zsobmon lovvi leddyx.

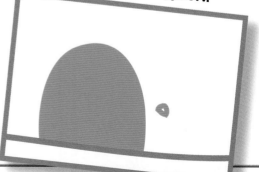

6 k zsq rsnsxq kbyexn k mybxob.

7 crkbu zkccsxq qkc.

8 yfobrokn fsog yp wkx gsdr k lkn mywl-yfob.

9 k byvvoblvknob yx k cukdolykbn.

10 mkwov gsdr k cokdlovd.

Use your decoder badges to find the answers. See page 405.

119

Is This the World's Lamest Trick?

There is a fine line between breathtaking lameness and breathtaking genius. This is a trick that teeters on that line, before falling squarely into the genius zone. As a result, we love this trick without apology. It is called…

1. You and your friend sit at a table.

2. Fill a glass with water and set it on the table.

3. Cover the glass with a hat.

4. Announce that you can drink all the water without touching the hat.

5. Go under the table and make a lot of slurping noises.

6. Come back out. Smile and wipe your mouth.

7. Your friend lifts the hat to prove you didn't do anything but go under the table and make stupid slurping noises.

8. Grab the glass of water and drink it.

P.S. Use a napkin if you're hatless.

I can drink this water without touching the hat.

3 Cover glass with hat.

4

7

8 Drink.

And wear it on your head

How to Make a Napkin Bikini Top

1

The yellow dots are the corners. Keep your eye on them.

2

Fold top edge and bottom edge… …into the middle.

6

The bottom two corners are touching the table.

7

Peel back the top two layers…

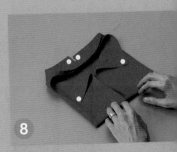

8

…to expose the bottom corners.

A nother fabulous way to spend that familiar time at the restaurant while you're waiting for your food. All you'll need is one of those cloth napkins and a willingness to step out there and make a fashion statement.

You can wear your bikini top in the conventional place or you can wear it on your head, like Nathan is doing here. Up to you.

3 Spin 90 degrees.

4 Lift...

5 ...at the middle.

9 Pick up all four corners...

10 ...and spread out.

11 Done.

How to Build a Plastic Spoon Catapult

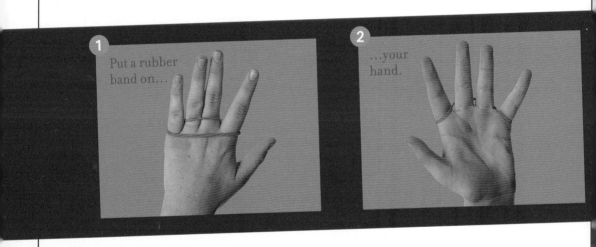

1 Put a rubber band on…

2 …your hand.

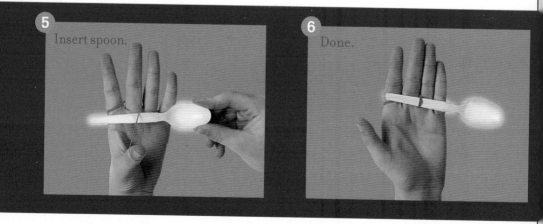

5 Insert spoon.

6 Done.

It has only been in the last few years that modern science has begun to take a serious look at plastic spoon catapults. Some of the newest designs combine performance and simplicity in a way that really sets a new standard. For example:

DID YOU KNOW?

A plastic spoon gripped in your teeth and loaded with ice cream is a ticket to Big Trouble.

3

Grab it here...

4

...and catch it with your thumb.

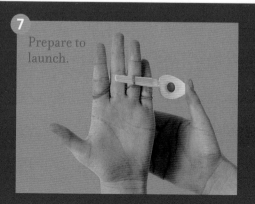

7

Prepare to launch.

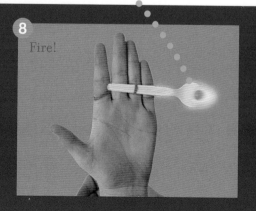

8

Fire!

How to Read a Shoe

Did you know you can actually read someone's fortune inside their shoe? Here are the simple-to-follow instructions:

Get your friend to give you their shoe. Close your eyes... look dreamy... rub the shoe and whisper the following words: **"It says here that you will soon be going... on... a... very... short... trip."**

Then throw the shoe over your shoulder... and run!

More Fridge Stickers

STOP!

BIOLOGICAL EXPERIMENT ☑ in progress ☐ finished

DO NOT OPEN THIS LABORATORY DOOR WITHOUT BACKUP

Cut out and tape to fridge door.

A CROW BOAT

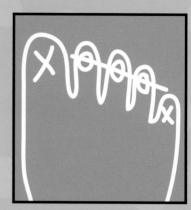

TIC-TAC-TOES

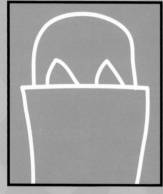

A CAT IN A BUCKET

What are these things?

A FLEASBURGER

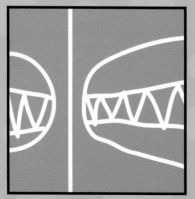

A T-REX LOOKING IN A MIRROR
TO SEE IF IT HAS ANY
STEGASAURUS IN ITS TEETH

PALM TREES

Rubber Band
Secret Messages

Here's a way to air-mail sensitive messages clear across entire classrooms and over the heads of nosy classmates and teachers. Only those who know the secret will be able to read them.

1 Stretch the rubber band as far as possible and get someone to hold it like that while you write your message.

← Grounded unjustly! Bring ladder to window tonight at 10! →

Stretched.

2 Let go of the rubber band. Presto! Secret message safe.

Grounded unjustly! Bring ladder to window tonight at 10!

Back to normal.

3 Launch across classroom.

Grounded unjustly! Bring ladder to window tonight at 10!

4 **S t r e t c h** to read.

How to Make a Personal Splatter Rainbow

The biggest problem with rainbows is they're never there when you need them.

At least, that used to be the problem. But that was before the invention of the *Personal Splatter Rainbow*, or PSR as it's sometimes called.

The instructions for making a PSR are quite simple. Just make sure you are outside standing with a bright sun low over your shoulder (avoid mid-day). You should either be by yourself, or with people who are already used to you.

1 Fill up your mouth entirely with water, full cheeks.

2 Then, suddenly squash your cheeks with your hands, shake your head violently, and splatter the whole mouthful in a fine mist directly in front of your face.

Your PSR will appear magically in front of you.
Repeat as necessary.

Are You a Southeye?

People tend to favor one eye over the other, just like they favor one hand over the other. (Although being a left-handed southpaw does not necessarily make you a southeye. There doesn't seem to be much connection between hands and eyes.)

Here's a quick test to see which eye you favor.

1 Hold your arm straight out and point at something in the distance.

2 Focus on the thing (not your finger).

3 Close one eye, then switch and close the other. One eye will make your finger jump, the other will not. When it does jump, the closed eye is your dominant eye.

BY THE WAY, WHAT'S YOUR BOSS THUMB?

Put your hands together like this, fingers laced together. Your dominant thumb is the one on top. Now switch thumbs and see if that doesn't feel weird.

Boss thumb.

Squeeze Bottle Thrill Machine

Wouldn't it be fun to have a special squeeze bottle by your kitchen sink that was loaded with a long white string? That way, whenever someone new comes into your kitchen, you're always ready. Pick it up and give it a good squeeze at point blank range! Won't your parents' guests be surprised when the string comes flying at them?

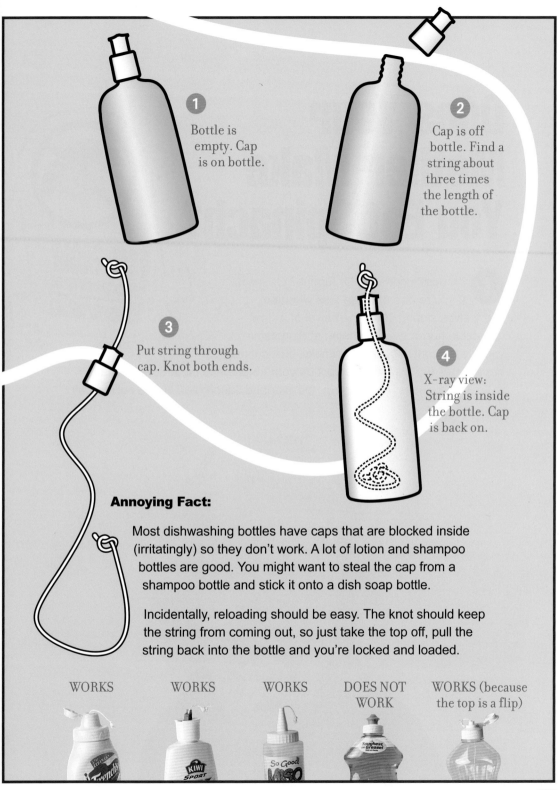

1 Bottle is empty. Cap is on bottle.

2 Cap is off bottle. Find a string about three times the length of the bottle.

3 Put string through cap. Knot both ends.

4 X-ray view: String is inside the bottle. Cap is back on.

Annoying Fact:

Most dishwashing bottles have caps that are blocked inside (irritatingly) so they don't work. A lot of lotion and shampoo bottles are good. You might want to steal the cap from a shampoo bottle and stick it onto a dish soap bottle.

Incidentally, reloading should be easy. The knot should keep the string from coming out, so just take the top off, pull the string back into the bottle and you're locked and loaded.

WORKS   WORKS   WORKS   DOES NOT WORK   WORKS (because the top is a flip)

Does Your Mother Make You Eat Spinach?

Or brussels sprouts? Or turnips? Or snails? If you're one of those kids who find themselves staring down the barrel of a new vegetable horror every evening at dinnertime, your life is about to get much simpler. Just cut out this *Vege-Proof Tongue Cover*, slap it on your tongue and bend down the tabs to keep it in place. Then bring on the liver and sauerkraut: You're bulletproof.

VEGE-PROOF TONGUE COVER

Silverware Somersaults

You are sitting at a restaurant table with other people. You are eating, or waiting for your food, or maybe everyone is just staring blankly at everyone else. In any event, you are NOT being amazing. How do you fix this picture?

1 Arrange two spoons and a cup as shown. Make sure the spoons overlap.

2 Then make everyone hush, take a deep breath, and suddenly whap where it says to. Do it right — not too hard and not too soft — and the spoon (or fork) will execute a beautiful single flip and drop into the glass.

Three points.

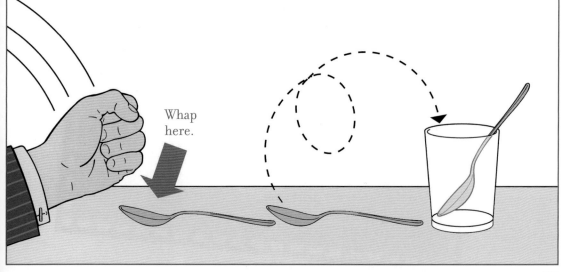

Whap here.

Cut it out

An Official Thumb Wrestling Mat

One, two, three, four, I declare a thumb war.

Insert thumb here

IF ANYONE TEARS THIS MAT, **THEY LOSE!**

Insert thumb here

Never Wait in Line Again

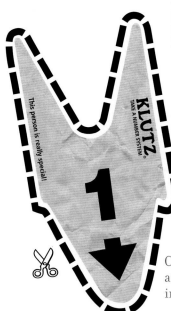

How would you like to be **Number 1** in line — every time? Just cut this little ticket out, put it in your wallet and whip it out whenever you need it! And remember! Your turn isn't next, your turn is NOW!

Cut out and keep in wallet.

This person is really special!

KLUTZ®
TAKE A NUMBER SYSTEM

1

Here's one for your friend.

This person is really special!

KLUTZ®
TAKE A NUMBER SYSTEM

419

Make a Tomato Goosh Monster

Sorry kids, but grown-ups have been right all these years. Vegetables ARE good; they're good for making tomato goosh monsters! Here's how to do it.

Turn a cherry tomato into a happy face by poking two eyes and cutting a little smile.

Hold your happy tomato up, show him around, let other people admire him ("So cute!") and then squeeze him from behind so that all the innards squeeze out of his eyes and mouth! Charming!

How Weird Is Your Tongue?

Are you ashamed of your tongue? Do you always change the subject when other people talk about theirs? If you do, we'd like to help! Fill out this questionnaire and tally up your points.

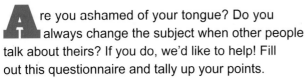

A TONGUE QUESTIONNAIRE

Fill in the blank: 1 for a NO; 2 for a YES.

_____ Can curl tongue into tube.

_____ Can stand tongue on one edge, then flip it over and stand it on the other.

_____ Can form the tip of tongue into a W.

_____ Can form a bubble on the end of tongue, and then blow it off, intact!

_____ TOTAL

4 = boring
5 = fairly normal
6 = a little weird
7 = pretty weird
8 = really weird

Be Still My Beating Heart

As your arms go down, your heart goes thump. It's amazing.

1 This sleeve is empty.

This sleeve has an arm in it.

2

3 Thump.

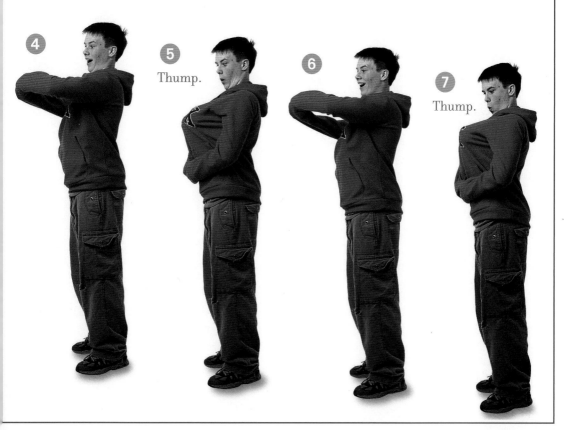

4

5 Thump.

6

7 Thump.

Great at the last minute

The Wet Dash Science Project

It's science fair season, and we're here to help with the best project we've ever heard of. In the *Run or Walk Rainy Day Science Project*, you get to run around in the rain wearing a sheet, and at the same time answer a burning scientific question, namely: If you have to walk across the street in the rain, is it better to run — or walk?

If you walk, you'll spend more time out in the rain. But if you run, you'll smack into a bunch of raindrops that you would have otherwise missed. You could program a supercomputer to do the math, or you and a friend could wrap yourselves in sheets, line up together at one end of a field on a really rainy day, and set off for the opposite side.

Walker   Runner

Important point: Somebody has to walk, somebody has to run. Immediately afterwards, take off the sheets, hang them on opposite ends of a balance stick, and see which sheet got wetter and so weighs more — runner or walker.

Runner

Walker

What Is the Second Verse to "Great Green Gobs"?

The following songs are sure to bring a smile to anyone… who cannot hear them. Sing loud and sing proud and sing again and again and again…

Great green gobs of greasy grimy gopher guts, Mutilated monkey meat, little dirty birdy feet. French-fried eyeball rolling in a pool of glub, and I forgot my spoo–oo–oon! (slurp!)

We three kings of Orient are. Tried to smoke a rubber cigar. It was loaded, It exploded, Scattering near and far... Ooooh Boom!

One dark day in the middle of the night, two bad boys got up to fight. Back to back they faced each other, drew their swords and shot each other. A deaf policeman heard the noise and came right out and got those boys.

Here Are Your Lifetime Goals

It's very annoying, but grown-ups (teachers especially) will sometimes want to know what your lifetime goals are. Well, starting right now, that's an easy question to answer. Your goals are to find these three amazing roadside rarities. It's your huge "lifetime scavenger hunt." Keep this scorecard in your wallet and whip it out whenever you get the annoying "lifetime goals" question.

MY LIFETIME GOALS ARE TO SPOT:

CLOWN IN CAR FULL OF BALLOONS

_____

place sighted   date

GIANT FAKE DINOSAUR

_____

place sighted   date

OSCAR MAYER WIENERMOBILE

_____

place sighted   date

School Supplies
Gone Crazy

Have you ever wondered what all that stuff in your pencil case is for?

The Paper Cup Honk Machine

With a wet sponge (or wet paper towel), slide your hand down the string while you hold the cup. It makes a loud squonking noise, exactly like a duck with a bad cold.

Knot

Paper cup (or plastic)

String, at least 12 inches long. Shoelace doesn't work.

Pull down firmly on string. Slide your hand down the string.

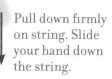

Read it out loud

Which Fairy Tale Is This?

Wants pawn term dare worsted ladle gull hoe lift wetter murder inner ladle cordage honor itch offer lodge, dock, florist. Disk ladle gull orphan worry putty ladle rat cluck wetter ladle rat hut, an fur disk raisin pimple colder Ladle Rat Rotten Hut.

Answer in back.

Yummy

Have a Footsicle!

Cut this out. Tape Popsicle® stick to the foot. Then coat the whole foot, both sides, with clear tape. Add Kool-Aid® to an empty ice cube tray. Insert foot into one of the compartments. Freeze and voilá: Footsicle.

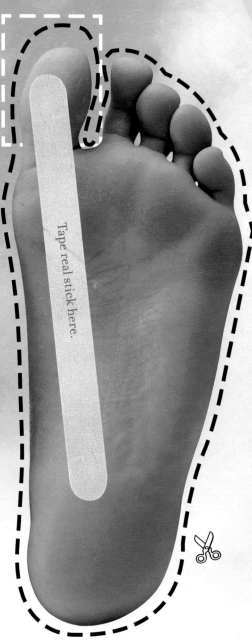

Tape real stick here.

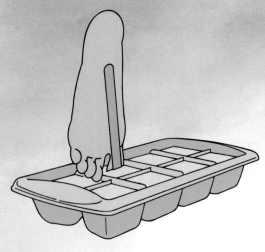

Comic Book Spelling Bee

Ask your English teacher how to spell the following words and then grade them!

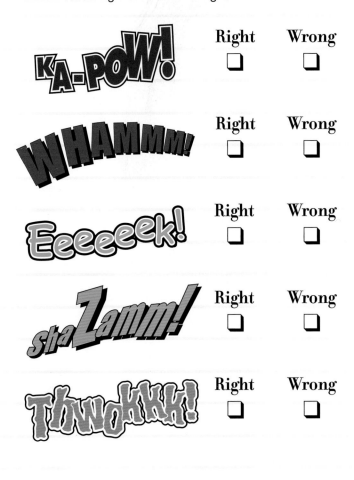

	Right	Wrong
K-A-POW!	☐	☐
WHAMMM!	☐	☐
Eeeeeek!	☐	☐
shaZamm!	☐	☐
Thwokkk!	☐	☐

For $1 Million, Tear Out This Page and Fold on the Dotted Line

Fold here.

Check that. Actually we need you to fold this page in half ten times — not just once. Other than that detail, the offer stands. Here's how to do it:

Tear this page out of the book and fold it in half. Then fold it in half again. Then do it again. And again. And again. And again. And again. And again. And again. And again.

The catch? It's impossible. A piece of paper can't be folded in half ten times. We hope.

Be a Stapler Artiste

If you are reading a page as sensitive and intelligent as this one, you undoubtedly have an enormous amount of artistic talent. At the same time, for the same reason, you're probably weary of ordinary artist's materials like paint and so forth.

Which is why we are providing you with an opportunity to explore stapler art, the exciting new medium everybody's talking about! Start by doing this stapler connect-the-dots, but don't stop there. Try landscapes, still lifes, portraits!

MEOW!

Put a staple between 1 and 2. Then another one between 3 and 4. Then another one between…

Do not back up!
Severe Brain Damage!

If you ignore this warning and read the following text backwards, you will experience severe brain pain, a strange sensation of faint nausea and lightheadedness. Please do not attempt to read the following backwards.

A nut for a jar of tuna.

A dog! A panic in a pagoda!

Rats live on no evil star.

Too hot to hoot.

I prefer pi.

The Universal Excuse Note

Photocopy about ten of these, fill in your name and put in your wallet. Use for the rest of your life.

URGENT MEMORANDUM

PLEASE EXCUSE _____

from _____ **today.**

He/she was detained on a sensitive matter of grave importance and international urgency. Thank you very much for your understanding.

G. Washington
George Washington

A. Einstein
Albert Einstein

Queen Elizabeth
Queen Elizabeth

FOUNDATION OF UNIVERSAL EXCUSES

Change Your Change

I t's amazing what a little nail polish (or permanent marker) can do for ordinary coins. The photos here are for inspiration, 12 ideas out of millions. Express yourself for 25 cents. Once you've tried a full color quarter, you'll never go back.

CLEAN UP THOSE PENNIES. Old pennies left overnight in a glass full of vinegar and salt will brighten right up.

Or at least look like it

Never Fall Asleep in Class Again!

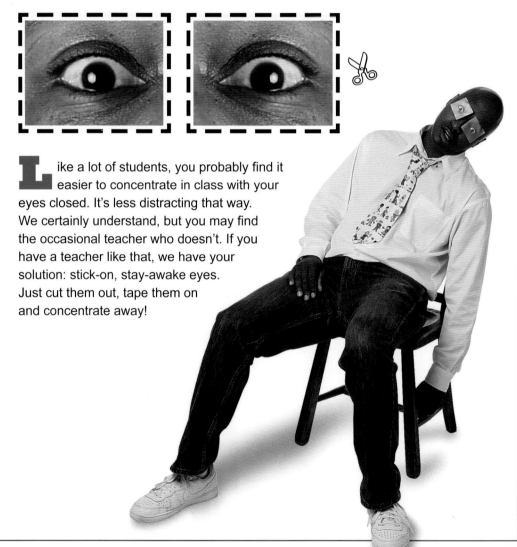

Like a lot of students, you probably find it easier to concentrate in class with your eyes closed. It's less distracting that way. We certainly understand, but you may find the occasional teacher who doesn't. If you have a teacher like that, we have your solution: stick-on, stay-awake eyes. Just cut them out, tape them on and concentrate away!

How to Turn F's into A's

When we were in 4th grade, friends often used to ask us how we were able to get such good grades, even though we sometimes didn't appear to work as hard as some of the other students. And teachers were always saying things to the class like, "There is no shortcut here. If you want to turn those F's into A's, you'll just have to buckle down. The secret to success is hard work."

That was a tough secret for us to crack, and we were still trying to figure it out when Dickie Rajoppi moved into our 4th grade class. Dickie sat next to us and Dickie, we discovered, had a far, far better secret, which he shared with us and which we will now share with you. You'll need a pen, and a quiet moment or two with your report card before your parents see it.

Incidentally, unlike a lot of systems that are supposed to help you improve your grades, our system is guaranteed.

Use a marker on the dotted line.

Before

After

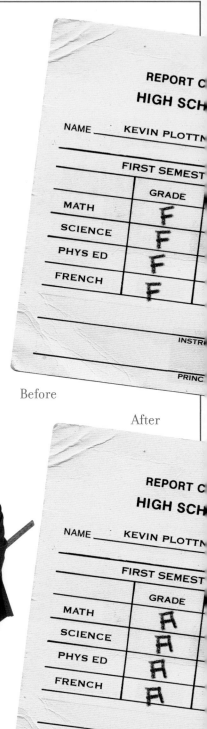

Before

After

REPORT C
HIGH SCH

NAME — KEVIN PLOTTN

FIRST SEMEST

	GRADE
MATH	F
SCIENCE	F
PHYS ED	F
FRENCH	F

INSTR

PRINC

REPORT C
HIGH SCH

NAME — KEVIN PLOTTN

FIRST SEMEST

	GRADE
MATH	A
SCIENCE	A
PHYS ED	A
FRENCH	A

INSTR

PRINC

Build a Bridge for Pennies

Welcome to the fast-growing world of penny stacking. We provide here a set of instructions for your basic 43-cent bridge, but there is much more out there (see the Web, as usual). No glue, no tape, no cheats. All you need are steady hands and a pocketful of pennies.

1 Build a tower like this one.

2 On top of THAT tower add three more pennies.

3 Then build a matching tower and connect the two as shown.

The Broom & Egg Whap

Only a very few tricks can actually change your life. *The Broom & Egg Whap* is one of them. We have been doing it for many years, and its power to awe and inspire is undiminished. Here is what it looks like: A raw egg is carefully perched on a cardboard tube, on a pie tin, over a glass of water. A broom is used to slam the pie tin away and the egg drops miraculously into the water. Maybe.

Challenge:

Drop the egg
into the water.
No touching.

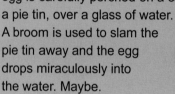

This man is
preparing to
slam the pie
tin away.

Ingredients

This is a broom.

One cardboard tube (like what comes from inside a toilet paper roll)

One real egg

One pie tin

One plastic glass half full of water

Egg in glass unbroken

Set up: Set the glass, pie tin, tube and egg on the edge of the table exactly as shown.

Line everything up…

Pie tin over-hangs edge of table by an inch.

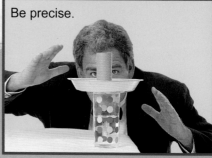

Be precise.

Place egg.

Hints:

- The glass isn't glass. It's plastic.
- The pie tin overhangs the edge of the table by an inch or so!
- Don't stick the egg into the tube. Just balance it.
- The tube is dead center over the glass.

Get ready: Cock the broom by tromping on the bristles and hauling back on the handle.

Put the broom exactly under the edge of the table.

1 Ready.

2 Set.

3 Release.

4 Egg in glass unbroken

Amazing success.

Haul back on the broom, make sure no one's going to get hit by all the flying stuff, and then let go. The egg will drop into the glass maybe 90% of the time. The rest of the time something even funnier happens — it misses and makes a mess.

And other classroom stalls

Do Little People Live on Atoms?

Whenever you have ten minutes left in the class, and the teacher still hasn't remembered to assign any homework, you have a huge opportunity. If you can buy ten lousy minutes, the bell of freedom will ring.

Here's how to seize that opportunity.

Distract her. Stick your hand up and ask some incredibly deep question that will involve the class in lively discussion. (At least it will if you pre-alert them…) Then, keep it going as the… minutes… tick… away.

Here are a few deep questions and their discussion points. Enough to get you started…

1 Do little people live on atoms? Have you ever noticed the amazing similarity between your average atom and our solar system? A bunch of little things whizzing around a big thing in the middle? Coincidence? And what IF little people DO live on atoms? What are THEY made of? MORE atoms! And who do you think lives on THOSE atoms? Huh? (You can take it from there…)

Hello.

2 **How come buttered toast always falls butter side down?**
Pretend the cover of your book has butter on it, then get everyone to be like real scientists and try an experiment. Get everyone to push their books to the edge of their desks so they all fall off at once. How many of them fell cover side up? Huh? 80% right? What's up with that? Re-do the experiment multiple times. Do it in slo-mo. Chart results. Discuss.

3 **If a tree falls in the forest, does it make any noise?** This is a classic, and the way to extend it is easy. Just get someone to raise their hand and say, "What tree? You can't hear it, you can't see it, maybe you can't even feel it?" (You can take it from there.)

4 **How come we have so many words for "vomit"?** You know how the Eskimos have thousands of words for snow? How come we have the same deal with throwing up? How many words are there? *Upchuck, heave, barf, toss cookies, spit up, retch* (get everyone to help… we thought of 20). Is "vomit" for us like "snow" is for Eskimos? Discuss.

5 **Do I own a little piece of China?** If gold is discovered under my house, it's mine, right? Even if it's really deep. Really, really, really deep? So deep, in fact, that it's on the backside of the planet? In other words, why can't I go to China and tell the guy who's living in the house opposite mine to get off my property? (Hint: Extend this discussion by wondering if airplanes over your house are "trespassing.")

Thou art a rank fly-bitten clack dish.

Thou art a pox-marked mammering hugger mugger.

Thou art a churlish beef-witted barnacle.

Shakespearean edition

Talk Trash with the Best

Thou art a paunchy common-kissing lewdster.

Thou art a craven boil-brained codpiece.

Shakespeare had a staggering collection of insults and is widely recognized as one of history's biggest meany mouths. He might call someone "a beslubbering clay-brained barnacle!" Or, "a fool-born, boil-brained measle!" And those were his friends! If you'd like to try a little Shakespearean trash talk, just connect the dots. Go from the words in the left column, to words in the middle column, to words in the right column. And then the next time someone irritates you, just stand up straight and say...

Thou art a spleeny folly-fallen bladder.

Thou art a gorbellied doghearted...

Thou art a puking gleeking flapdragon.

...ering	beef-witted	barnacle
bootless	beetle-headed	bladder
churlish	boil-brained	boar-pig
craven	common-kissing	canker-blossom
currish	crook-pated	clack-dish
dankish	dismal-dreaming	clotpole
droning	doghearted	codpiece
fawning	earth-vexing	dewberry
fobbing	elf-skinned	flap-dragon
froward	fat-kidneyed	flax-wench
gleeking	flap-mouthed	foot-licker
goatish	fly-bitten	fustilarian
gorbellied	folly-fallen	giglet
lumpish	hasty-witted	horn-beast
mammering	hedge-born	hugger-mug er
mangled	hell-hated	joithead
mewling	idle-headed	lewdster
paunchy	ill-breeding	lout
pribbling	ill-nurtured	maggot-
puking	knotty-pated	malt-w n
puny	milk-livered	ma t
qualling	motley-mi	r e
rank	oni	
reeky	plu	
ruttish	pox-m	
spleeny	rough-hewn	

Thou art a dankish idle-headed foot-licker.

In a single-story house

How to Walk Down Stairs

Seen from
the front

Seen from
the back

Webcams and fancy camera cell phones have created some tempting opportunities for homemade special FX. Check out the pictures below for an example of how you might perform your own stunts in a home-improvement film you could call *The Basement of Your Dreams*.

Trip, Stumble and Clonk

Buying a big red nose and learning nothing but these two skills will get you into some of the most selective clown schools in the country.

How to Trip on a Curb. As you approach the curb, kick it and do a fake stumble over it. Immediately go into the next bit…

4

5

THIS WAY TO THE WALL

6

Clonk Your Head on a Wall

After you've "tripped" on the curb, stagger towards a lamppost or wall. Then, just before you walk straight into it, kick it loudly and "bounce" back, holding your forehead and moaning.

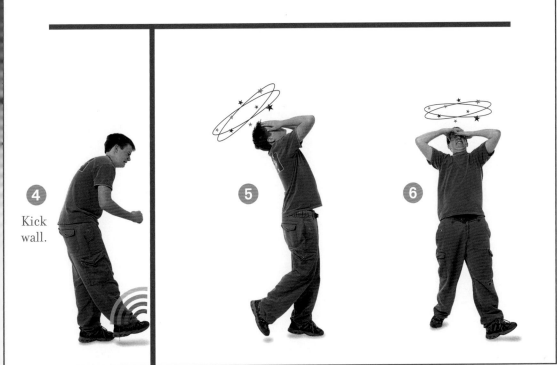

4
Kick
wall.

5

6

How to Bite Off Your Finger

When you think about things to be when you grow up, have you ever considered cannibal? A lot of kids these days wait too long before making these key career decisions, and oftentimes, they end up making hurried lifelong mistakes as a result. If cannibal is on your list of "maybe's" here's a way to test-drive the idea before you commit. Think of it as a way to take a small bite.

1 Insert forefinger in mouth and begin gnawing on it. Gently.

2 Remove and inspect.

3 Repeat two more times... Gnaw...

4 Remove and inspect.

5 Finally, as you insert it for the fourth time, bend it at the knuckle at the instant it goes in. Then, with a huge grimace, fake chomp it off. Chew for a while – don't forget there's a bone in there – and finally swallow. Hold up your hand with the finger bent out of sight, smile a bit and... burp.

Are you a stickler for accuracy? Crunch some ice right here.

Drinking ketchup

A Fast Food Switcheroo

Here we go again, getting out there on the ragged edge. As we have stated before, we don't go in for pranks that leave scars. However, this one is right on the line. We will describe it and allow your own good taste to decide on which side it falls.

1 **You're at a fast food place.** Your friend has left to go to the bathroom or somewhere. Or maybe you're bringing his food from the counter. In any event, you are left alone and unsupervised with the food. This is your opportunity, and his mistake.

2 Quickly drink down your own Coke® and then take off the lid. Stick the bottom end of the straw into one of those ketchup packets.

3 Replace lid and switch drinks. Your work here is done.

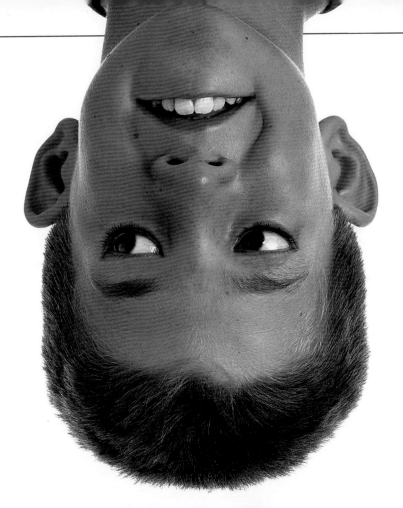

Anything Wrong with Brad?

This is one of our favorite optical illusions. If you can't figure out what's wrong by staring at the picture, just flip it over. The answer will become very clear, trust us.

How to Whistle with Your Fingers

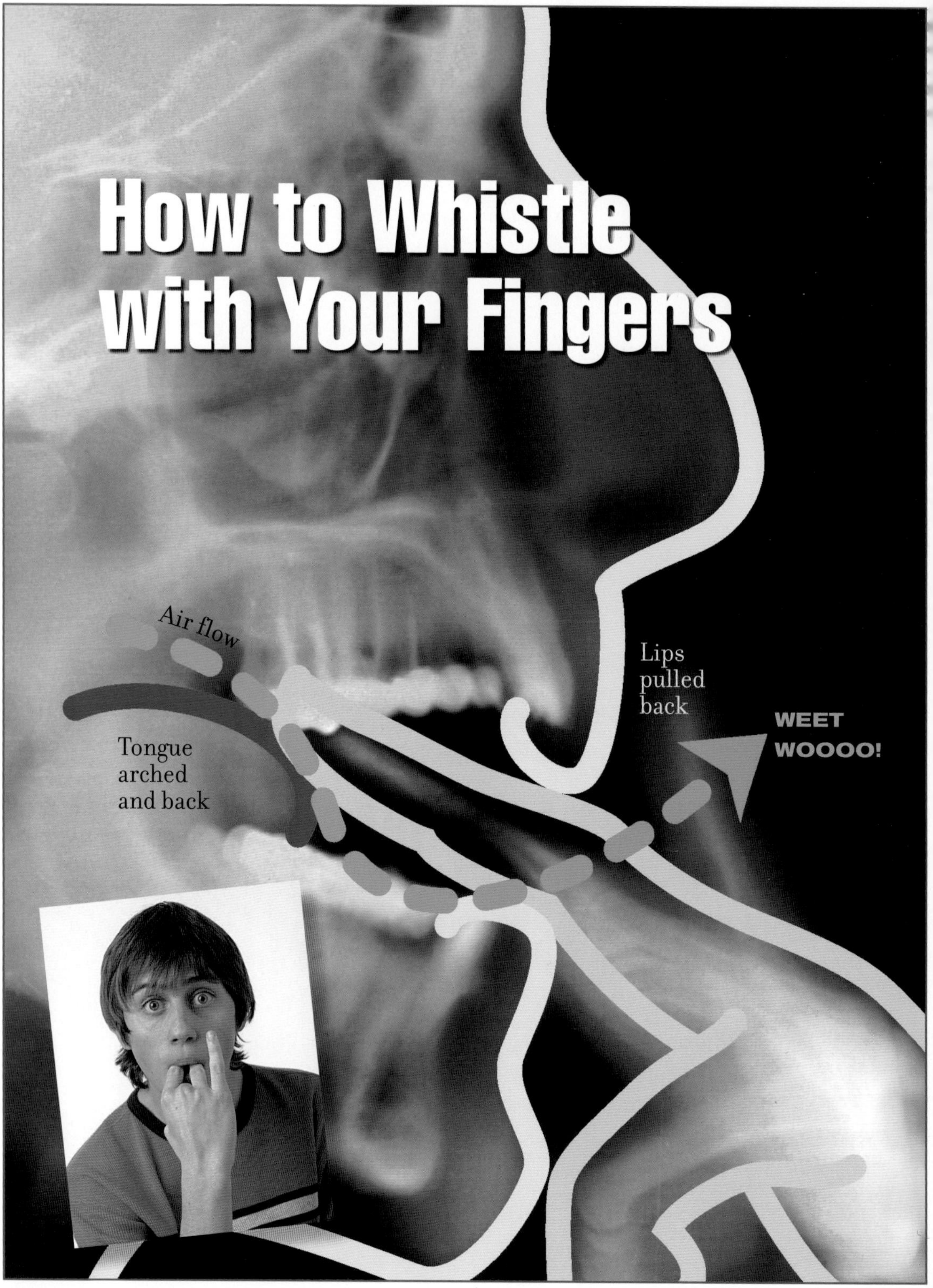

Air flow

Lips
pulled
back

Tongue
arched
and back

**WEET
WOOOO!**

We come now to an important, but difficult, lesson. "Important" because no properly educated kid should grow up in these modern high-tech times without learning how to blow an ear-piercing whistle. "Difficult" because it takes practice and learning is all frustration by trial and error. No one is going (or is willing) to hold your hand while you learn. That's just gross. Sorry.

Look at the X-ray for the idea. You will be pushing back on the tip of your tongue. Don't push it all the way to the back of your mouth, just about halfway. We use the forefinger and ringfinger, but others use the thumb and forefinger or even both pinkies. Use whatever feels comfortable for you. Make a choice and go with it.

Push the tip of your tongue back, then cover your upper teeth with your upper lip. Look at the pictures to see how far you should push your fingers in and what kind of an angle you should use.

Fool with the angle while you blow lightly. Listen for the hollow sound you get when you blow over the top of a bottle. That's your signal that you're getting close.

Once you've found the hollow sound, keep blowing and keep fooling with the angle (little tiny changes make big differences).

Don't practice for long periods. Do it in short, 1-minute bursts. And work in the zone where you hear a hollow sound. Practice frequently, while you're standing in line or just waiting around. Nobody learns this quickly! It might take a while, but Huckleberry Finn and Tom Sawyer could both do it, and so can you.

You can hold your fingers this way…

…this way…

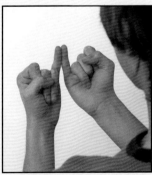

…or this way.

How to Whistle with Your Hands

This is another kid skill that should be a basic part of never growing up. It takes a little practice, but if you attack the problem with frequent, short sessions, you'll get much less frustrated. Do it for a few seconds a few times every day. Keep in mind the key points and fool with the process. Once you get it, you'll never go back.

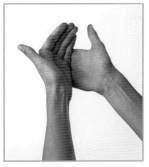

1 Shape your hands into a cave as shown.

2 It should be tight enough to hold water.

The door to your cave

3 The door to the cave is formed by your thumbs.

Blow across the door to your cave…

…It's like blowing across the opening of a bottle.

Put the "door" to your lips as shown. And blow ACROSS it, <u>not</u> into it. When you hear a hollow sort of sound, you are getting warm. Fool with your angles and the shape of your door.

Little changes make big differences. Keep at it. Remember that the "hollow sound" is your "getting warmer" sign. Never practice for more than a minute or two; it's too frustrating otherwise. And don't forget! Blow ACROSS the door — not into it. It's exactly like making a bottle hoot.

Test Your Driver

You might be interested in learning how your driver tests on the following questions. Since you're in the car with him or her all the time, and since it's probably been a little while since they took driver's ed, it only seems prudent to find out what they remember. We're talking your safety here, so it's hard to be too careful. Here are the questions you should ask them.

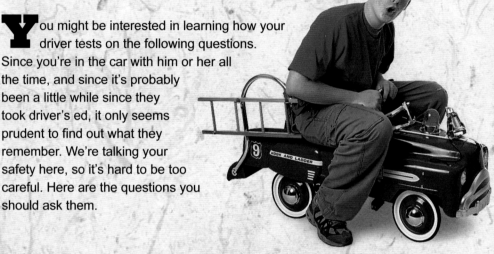

Is it safer to drive at night or daytime?	❑ Night ☒ Day ❑ Same
You're driving on a four-lane road. An emergency vehicle is approaching you from the opposite direction. What do you do?	❑ Pull over ☒ Get in the far right lane ❑ Turn around and follow him
The green light is at the	❑ Top of a stoplight ☒ Bottom of a stoplight
A balloon is hanging mid-air in your car. You're stopped. Then you hit the gas hard. The balloon goes...	☒ Forward ❑ Backwards ❑ Nowhere

Q: A volcano is exploding behind you. How fast do you have to leave the scene?

A: Very quickly. This jeep made it because it was far enough away. Up close, the cloud of super-heated ash moves at 400 mph.

Q: What's the most dangerous state to drive in? With the highest accident rate per passenger-mile? New York, California, Virginia, Arizona or Wyoming?

A: Wyoming

Q: Are smelly cardboard pine trees hanging off the rearview mirror illegal?

A: Yes. You can't obscure the windshield with anything but a government-issued sticker.

Q: All the cars in North America averaged 22.1 mpg in 1997. In 2005, they averaged more, less or the same.

A: Less. [21 mpg]

Q: Where did the steel in your car come from?

A: Most likely from old cars, since recycled steel is the norm in car building these days.

Bounce a Dughnut

The next time you're at the dinner table and they serve rolls, cupcakes, muffins, cookies, bagels, doughnuts (or whatever), pick one up and throw it hard to the ground at your feet. It'll bounce high over your head, allowing you to catch it and take a bite.

Throw the doughnut to the floor.

What it looks like

What's really happening

Note: Foot is ready to stamp.

Actually, to be more accurate, that is what it'll look like to anyone sitting across the table from you. What they won't see (if you do it right) is the fact that you've stamped your foot to get the sound of the bounce at just the right instant. To get the bounce you toss the doughnut from out of view, below the table. See the pictures for a better idea.

It bounces. You can hear it.

4

It pops up…

5

…and you catch it.

6

This is the key step. Foot stamps. Turn hand over and flip doughnut into air. Keep it all under the table, invisible.

Getting ready to catch.

Grass Shrieking

Hold a blade of grass as shown between your thumbs. Press it to your mouth and blow through it hard. If you're lucky, and hold the grass tight, you will create a very loud and irritating noise.

(Helpful hint: If you're having trouble, ask the kid next to you for help, or if you're desperate, maybe even your parent. Grass shrieking is known by the ancients.)

Modern variation:
Cellophane works as well as grass. Probably even better.

Challenge! If you think you're good at this already, try it with a strip of regular paper. It can be done. We've seen it.

Mouth goes here.
Blow hard.

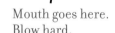

How to Stick a Finger Through Your Head

1 Point your finger into your ear.

2 Jam it through your eardrum. Done.

3 NO! WAIT! This is a trick! Make it LOOK like you've jammed your finger through your eardrum by bending it away from your audience and simultaneously sticking your tongue into your cheek.

Be really irritating

Make a Mouse Blinder

People often ask us the same question: "Dear Klutz," they'll write, "I'd love to be really irritating and obnoxious, but I just don't have the time anymore. Is there some way I can really annoy people, without having to go to a lot of effort?"

This is a huge problem in these busy times we all live in. Fortunately, we have the answer. Make a *Mouse Blinder* out of a yellow stickie note! It's really easy! And it's really annoying!

1 Put a sticky note on the bottom of your friend's computer mouse, so the little light is covered, or the little ball can't roll. Now his computer won't work, no matter what he says to it.

2 Actually, there isn't a step two. You're done. Your friend will fuss around for hours trying to re-boot or call the computer company. Fun for almost everyone!

And other body parts

How to Thread Your Fingers

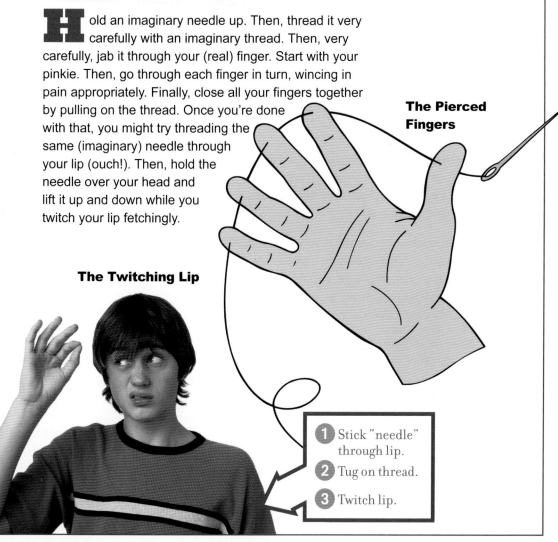

Hold an imaginary needle up. Then, thread it very carefully with an imaginary thread. Then, very carefully, jab it through your (real) finger. Start with your pinkie. Then, go through each finger in turn, wincing in pain appropriately. Finally, close all your fingers together by pulling on the thread. Once you're done with that, you might try threading the same (imaginary) needle through your lip (ouch!). Then, hold the needle over your head and lift it up and down while you twitch your lip fetchingly.

The Pierced Fingers

The Twitching Lip

1 Stick "needle" through lip.

2 Tug on thread.

3 Twitch lip.

Do You Have a Weird Face?

A lot of people think they can make a weird face, and of course they're very proud of that. We've all met the type. Just because they can cross their eyes and stick out their tongue, suddenly they think they're touching greatness.

It's laughable, of course. A truly great weird face is not something that just anyone can do. Leading scientists have identified only a very limited number of truly great weird faces, faces so special that they have actually been catalogued and given specific names.

Here, as it currently stands, are the top six weird faces. Don't be discouraged if you can't do any of them. The photographs here are of professional models doing faces that they have trained extensively for. Please, for safety's sake, don't try any of them at home.

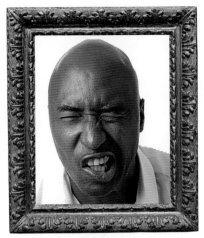

WANGOO

BUG-EYED BLOW BEETLE

PUCKER PUSS

SQUINTASTICO

SHOCK-A-TOLA

THE McFWIZZ

Clip These Articles

Tear these authoritative articles out. Show to parents.

Leading Scientists Revise Food Pyramid

PALO ALTO — New research has recently led many leading scientists to revise the familiar food pyramid we all learned as school children. "Frankly, some of the findings really surprised us," remarked one of the scientists, "especially the importance of convenience store food." What follows is the revised food pyramid for the new century. We suggest you post it on your refrigerator and look at it whenever you feel tempted by a big bowl of spinach or kale.

Licorice Rope Food Group
For example: red, black, etc.

The Secret Fillings Food Group
Anything that has a "Surprise Inside!" For example: packaged cupcakes, vending machine fruit pies, jelly doughnuts, etc.

Convenience Store Food Group
For example: packaged burritos or sandwiches, hot dogs, Slurpee® drinks, etc.

The Squirt Can Food Group
Anything that can be squirted from a can. For example: whipped cream, cheese whizzy stuff, etc.

Their is justice.

President Signs "Fair Spelling" Law

They're = Their = There

WASHINGTON — The President signed a new bill into law today that legalizes a number of new spellings. On hand at the Rose Garden ceremony was a huge crowd of students who cheered as the President misspelled his name.

Under the terms of the new law, which becomes effective today, the following spellings are now legal and can be used whenever you like.

they're = their = there (all are fine anywhere)

the = teh

two = too = to

kat = cat

you're = your

it's = its

Stockings for Naughty Kids

Like most of the kids who are reading this book, you've probably been mostly perfect this year. You're on Santa's "nice" list and you're expecting a pretty good haul this holiday season.

Congratulations! But don't you feel bad for all those other kids, like your siblings maybe, who haven't been as good as you?

Of course you do! That's what makes you "nice." Here's what you can do: Just cut out this stocking and give it to some bad kid you know so they can stick it to their mantel. Tell them: "Hey! Even bad kids like you deserve something!"

Cut along dotted line. Tape the two halves together. Leave the top open. Put on mantel.

You Bet Your Bicycle

All you need is a rope and a bike to pull this off. Get someone to stand beside the bike and balance it while you tie a rope to the pedal when it's at the bottom. Then, get behind the bike and pull. What do you think happens? Which way does the bike go? And which way does the pedal go?

We would of course love to give you the answer, but we don't want to rob you of the thrill of discovery. Try it yourself. We've done it a number of times and we still don't believe it.

This kid pulls rope.

This kid balances bike. She doesn't keep it from rolling.

Tie rope to pedal. Pull. Does bike go this way? Or this way?

The Round-the-Head Bubblegum Miracle

What would you think if a friend of yours were able to spit out a piece of gum, make it zoom around their head in a single orbit, and then zing it back into their mouth? No hands.

You'd be impressed, wouldn't you?

Well, guess what. They can't. But, if you have really long hair, and practice faithfully — you can. Select a single hair from the very top of your head, leave it in place, but chew the unattached end into your gum (which is still in your mouth, by the way). Then, spit it out hard enough so that it goes swinging around your head and pops back into your mouth after one complete, amazing orbit. (Yes, it takes practice, but miracles never come easy.)

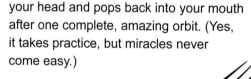

Hold straw like this. Pinch the ends airtight. Pinch real hard.

Popping Straws

Yet another restaurant item. You'll need a plastic straw and a partner. Grab the straw tightly at both ends, wind it up so the middle is bulging with compressed air. Then, get your partner to thump it. Your reward: a satisfying…

BANG!

Move your hands up and down like feet pedaling a bicycle to wind up the straw and compress the bulge.

Prepare to thump.

Straw will be shorter and bulging with compressed air.

How to Break Your Neck

In this frustrating world we all live in, knowing how to break your neck can really come in handy. Here are the easy-to-follow instructions.

1. When no one is looking, stick an empty water bottle in your armpit. Keep it hidden.

2. Then, gather a crowd, and proceed to twist and jerk your head around by grabbing it with both hands. Explain that you are doing a self-chiropractic thing since you have a little crick you're trying to get rid of.

3. At just the right moment, when you've got your head maximally torqued, crush the bottle under your arm so that it makes this horrible cracking sound and freeze your head. Say the words "Call a doctor." Very quietly.

Hide empty uncapped water bottle in armpit.

Carve a Barfkin

Have you ever wondered what to do with all the stuff that's inside your pumpkin? Answer: Just leave it there!

Be a Rubber Band Ninja Warrior

Do you scare people? When you drop into a ninja death crouch and growl, do your friends just ignore you? Or maybe even laugh? Would you like to change this picture?

Here's How

Find a fatty rubber band that fits kind of snugly around your head. Place it as shown. Carefully push it up until you start to feel it move on its own towards the top of your head. Immediately drop into your ninja crouch, growl and shift around until the rubber band makes its final slide up. Unless you're bald, at the very top of your head it should grab a samurai topknot of hair. At that instant, make a horrible face and freeze into your most menacing pose.

Some rubber bands work, some don't. A little flour on the band makes it slipperier, too.

Works.   **Doesn't.**

1 Find a fat rubber band.

2 Place on head as shown, at hairline (above forehead).

3 It should start to crawl up your head on its own.

4 Ninja!

Release the Prisoners

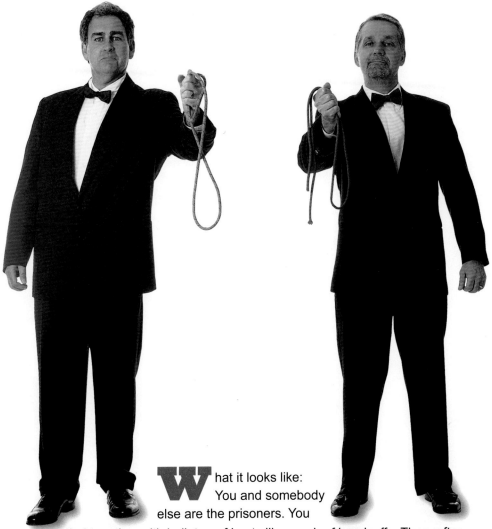

What it looks like: You and somebody else are the prisoners. You are tied together with bulletproof knots like a pair of handcuffs. Then, after wrestling around for a magical moment, you step free. Knots untouched.

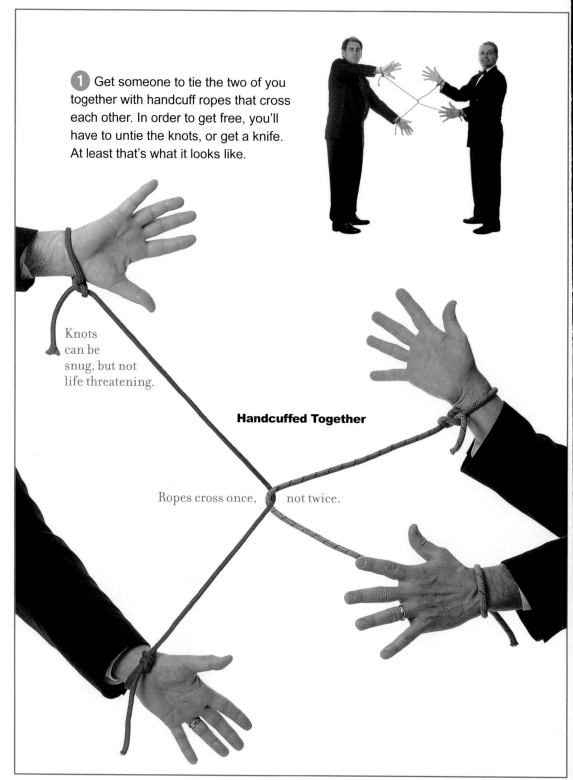

1 Get someone to tie the two of you together with handcuff ropes that cross each other. In order to get free, you'll have to untie the knots, or get a knife. At least that's what it looks like.

Knots can be snug, but not life threatening.

Handcuffed Together

Ropes cross once, not twice.

2 You and your fellow prisoner should now fall to the ground and wrestle around in a dogpile. Then, after a minute or two of that, you should untangle yourselves and step back...

...free at last!

P.S. Want the secret? Keep reading.

THE SECRET

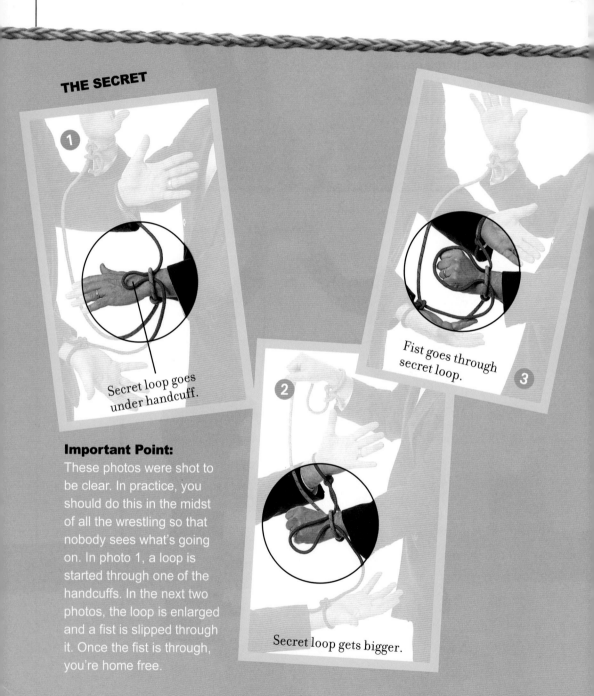

1 Secret loop goes under handcuff.

2 Secret loop gets bigger.

3 Fist goes through secret loop.

Important Point:
These photos were shot to be clear. In practice, you should do this in the midst of all the wrestling so that nobody sees what's going on. In photo 1, a loop is started through one of the handcuffs. In the next two photos, the loop is enlarged and a fist is slipped through it. Once the fist is through, you're home free.

Note: If you don't follow these photos carefully, you will push the loop through the handcuff wrong and when you step "free," you won't be. You'll still be stuck, maybe even double stuck. So pay attention.

⑤

...pull out.

④

Done.

The tricky part is all done. Now all you have to do is...

Free at last!

More no-practice magic

How to Bend the Silverware

How would you like to bend your mother's expensive silverware? Right before her thrilled and disbelieving eyes?

It's quite simple. You'll need your bare hands, a dime, and a lying tongue. Plus a fork.

The Set-Up

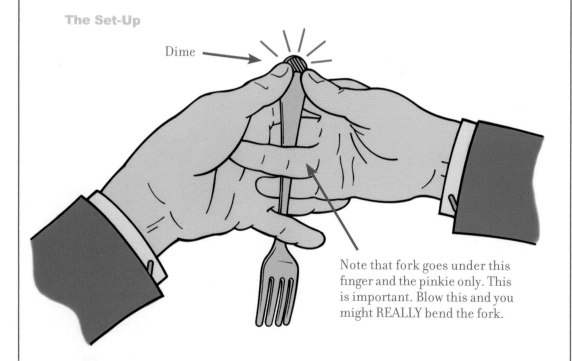

Dime →

Note that fork goes under this finger and the pinkie only. This is important. Blow this and you might REALLY bend the fork.

What Your Audience Sees

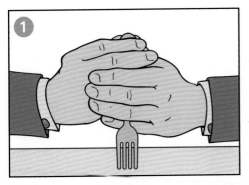

1 Put the prongs of the fork on the tabletop…

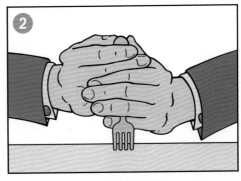

2 …and grunt as you "bend" it.

What You're <u>Really</u> Doing

1 Put the prongs of the fork on the tabletop…

2 …and grunt as you keep the dime in place and let the fork…

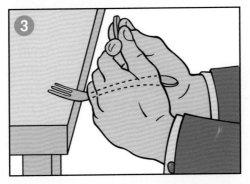

3 …slide between your hands.

Hey, Kids!

How Weird Are You?

You do this page.

Crack Knuckles
❏ Can (5 pts.)
❏ Can't

Lift Single Eyebrow
❏ Can (5 pts.)
❏ Can't

Form Tip of Tongue into "W" Shape
❏ Can (10 pts.)
❏ Can't

Ear Wiggling (true ear wiggling, not jaw wiggling that moves ears)
❏ Can (10 pts.)
❏ Can't

Can Burp Talk
❏ Can (4 pts.)
❏ Can't

Flip Eyelids Back
❏ Can (8 pts.)
❏ Can't

Bend Joint of Forefinger into Right Angle
❏ Can (6 pts.)
❏ Can't

Sneer on Both Sides of Mouth (in turn)
❏ Can (10 pts.)
❏ Can't

TOTAL UP YOUR POINTS. THIS IS YOUR OFFICIAL **WEIRD FACTOR.**

And How Weird Is Your Friend?

Your friend does this page.

Crack Knuckles
- ❏ Can (5 pts.)
- ❏ Can't

Lift Single Eyebrow
- ❏ Can (5 pts.)
- ❏ Can't

Form Tip of Tongue into "W" Shape
- ❏ Can (10 pts.)
- ❏ Can't

Ear Wiggling (true ear wiggling, not jaw wiggling that moves ears)
- ❏ Can (10 pts.)
- ❏ Can't

Can Burp Talk
- ❏ Can (4 pts.)
- ❏ Can't

Flip Eyelids Back
- ❏ Can (8 pts.)
- ❏ Can't

Bend Joint of Forefinger into Right Angle
- ❏ Can (6 pts.)
- ❏ Can't

Sneer on Both Sides of Mouth (in turn)
- ❏ Can (10 pts.)
- ❏ Can't

TOTAL UP YOUR POINTS. THIS IS YOUR OFFICIAL WEIRD FACTOR.

Make a Note Card Annoyer

Here's a great way to make a really annoying noise with nothing but a piece of paper about the size of a 3 x 5 notecard.

Look at the pictures to fold and cut the paper. Then hold it tightly in front of your mouth with two fingers and blow into it (with your mouth, not your nose) and fuss around until you get it to make this really nasty honking sound. Success!

HONK!

1 Fold a scrap of paper in half. Any kind of paper will work.

2 Cut two small notches on the fold.

3 Fold each half in half again.

4 Hold the noisemaker between your hands, as shown in the photograph. Place it over your lips and blow, keeping your lips close together. It may take a minute to get the hang of it, but you'll know when you do. Trust us.

Be an alien! In seconds!

In a Hurry This Halloween?

A lot of kids are so busy doing homework these days that they just don't have time to get ready for Halloween like they used to. We certainly understand and that's why we're here to help!

1. Get two cardboard toilet paper tubes.

2. Get someone to stick them onto your ears as shown. Use tape to hold them.

3. Then roll two tin foil antennae and attach to a hairband. **Wow!**

We Control Your Foot

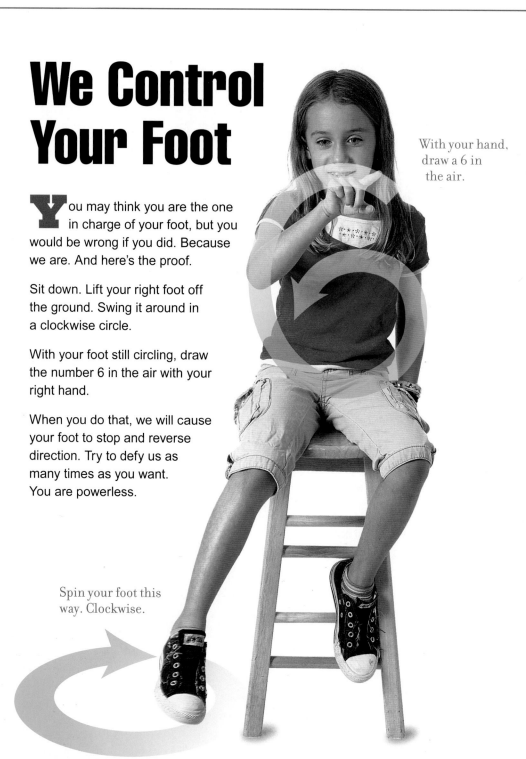

You may think you are the one in charge of your foot, but you would be wrong if you did. Because we are. And here's the proof.

Sit down. Lift your right foot off the ground. Swing it around in a clockwise circle.

With your foot still circling, draw the number 6 in the air with your right hand.

When you do that, we will cause your foot to stop and reverse direction. Try to defy us as many times as you want. You are powerless.

With your hand, draw a 6 in the air.

Spin your foot this way. Clockwise.

214

Static Electrickery

This is a very effective easy-to-do magic trick provided you're not bothered by the need to tell big fat lies.

Find a tapered pen cap.* Hold it as shown and squeeze it between your (wetted) fingers like a watermelon seed. It will fly away. Hold the pen right in the flight path and the cap will snap back into place magically.

1

Hold the cap between your fingers as shown and explain to everyone how pens are always negatively charged, and caps are always positive (this is a lie, incidentally).

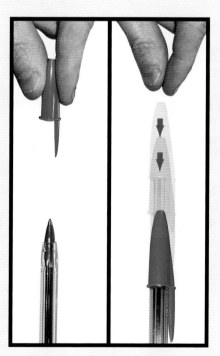

2

Then squeeze the cap like a watermelon seed and snap it onto the pen from an inch or two away. (This takes a little practice.)

Just amazing!

And do not give the secret away.

*Cap has to be tapered. No substitutions.

The Study Guide to the Study Guides

As a modern, hard-working student living in today's modern, fast-paced world, you know how valuable your limited time is. And so do we! That's why we've invented a new kind of study aid. We call them the *Notes to the Notes.* Because who has the time to read the whole Notes anymore?

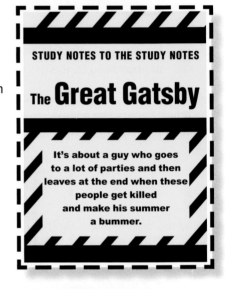

STUDY NOTES TO THE STUDY NOTES

The Great Gatsby

It's about a guy who goes to a lot of parties and then leaves at the end when these people get killed and make his summer a bummer.

STUDY NOTES TO THE STUDY NOTES

Moby Dick

It's about a big fish who kills a guy at the end.

STUDY NOTES TO THE STUDY NOTES

Hamlet

It's about this very depressive guy who gets upset when his father dies and his mom marries his uncle.

Backscratch Battleship

What would happen if you cross-bred the game of Battleship with a back rub? We tried it recently and discovered a strange and wonderful thing. We call it *Backscratch Battleship* and here is how it goes:

Both players (mentally) put this grid on their backs. On a piece of paper they write the secret location of their battleship. (For example, **B-2**.)

Then, players take turns scratching their opponent's squares to see who can be the first to sink a battleship.

You missed.
Try again — a
little lower
and harder.

Don't really
draw on
your shirt.
Just imagine.

On a real piece of paper,
draw your grid and black
out your battleship squares.

For complete beginners

How to Make a Lunchroom Bang

Making loud noises in the cafeteria or lunchroom is an activity that goes back to the dawn of time, back when loud noises were first invented.

Here are the five systems in common use today: the brown bag system, the CapriSun® or juice box system, as well as the more traditional milk carton and plastic Ziploc® sandwich bag systems. They all work, of course. It's just a matter of personal preference and what your mother gave you that morning.

The Brown Bag System

1 Inflate.　　**2** Wind up.　　**3** Bang!

The Plastic Bag System

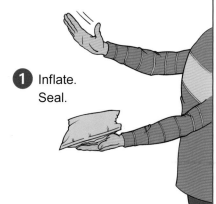

1 Inflate.
Seal.

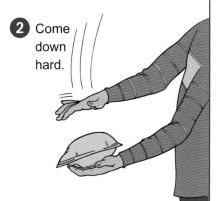

2 Come
down
hard.

The Juice Bag, Juice Box, Milk Carton System

1 Locate foot over inflated container.

2 Stomp.

3

Bang!

Modern hieroglyphs

Think Like an Egyptian

Connect each of these real symbols that appear on real signs with one of these captions that are entirely made up, but we think make sense anyway.

Fill in the letter:

_____ Looks Like a Puzzling Case to Me

_____ Leaning Tower of Puppy

_____ Insomniacs Club of America

_____ No Kicking Allowed

_____ Very Short Railroad

_____ Shocking News Enclosed

_____ Black Olive Snorters Society

_____ Elevator Out of Order

_____ You Left Your Backpack on the Roof

_____ Who's That Sleeping in My Bed?

_____ Who Am I?

_____ Friendly Giant Will Push Cars in Case of Emergency

Answers in back.

A

B

C

D

E

F

G

H

I

J

K

L

Misspell Your Name!

Most spelling bees make a really big deal out of spelling words correctly. Here at Klutz, we do knot. People who only know how to spell a word one way, we believe, lack imagination. That's why we are staging the world's first Misspelling Bee right here. The challenge? Misspell the letters in your name to improve it a lot.

Put your new, better spelling here.

Examples

~~George Gerston~~	Gorge Grrrrrstun
~~Phillip Smith~~	Fillup Smooth
~~Jake Morrissey~~	Joke Mororlessy
~~Rick Bodin~~	Brick Rodent
~~Mike Dowson~~	Muke Doofus
~~Alice Jones~~	Alias Bones

Drop me a shoe
Flip-Flop Mail

Flip-flops make lovely postcards —
no packaging necessary! Write
your message on the bottom and put the
stamps and address on the top. You have
to add extra postage to cover the hand-
canceling, but we've gotten flip-flop
messages through the mail and been
deeply moved.

You could probably do the same with
tennis shoes, although you'd have to
remove the laces and stinky insoles
first. Plus, you'd have to staple the
stamps since tape is a no-no over
stamps. Try it.

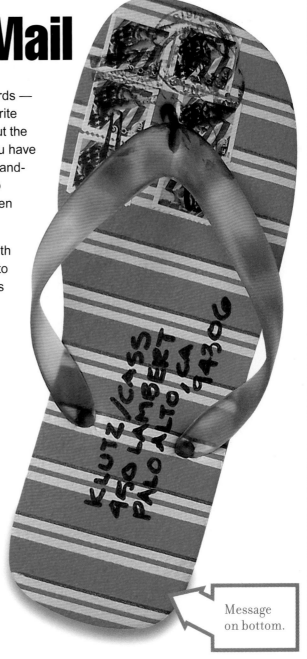

This shoe went through the mail
no problem. New York to Palo Alto.

Message
on bottom.

Make a Dead Leg

Cut off pant leg.

Dead legs are one of those rare accessories that go well with just about everything. Stick them out from under a dumpster, a desk, a car or an easy chair. Or, best of all, try this: Slam your trunk down on it so the foot sticks out. Then let your parents drive off without a clue. Hysterical!

There are a couple of ways to make a dead leg. One, you can take a rusty saw to your own leg, cut it off and use that. Or — and this is the system WE recommend — stuff an old pair of pants with rags or paper. Then pin on a shoe and sock. Done!

Stuff sock with paper.

Put stuffed sock in shoe.

Cover with pant leg.

Duct tape it all together.

The Mid-Air Reversing Ball Trick

This is an amazing demonstration of physics, mystery, psychology and true, true lameness.

Hold a ball in your hand. Allow your audience to hand it around. "Look it over very carefully. An absolutely normal ball." Then take it back and announce that you are going to throw this ball very hard. "Just as you'd expect, it will zoom away from my hand at great speed. But then — and this it where it gets really weird — in mid-air, it will stop, reverse direction AND THEN RETURN DIRECTLY TO MY HAND!"

People will not believe you. Smile mysteriously. Wind up with great effort… and toss it straight up into the air and catch it.

And run.

Dumb Dialogue Bubbles

Cut these out and stick onto photos in your yearbook. Makes a huge improvement.

"Some of my hair is real!"

"All these people smell funny."

"I'm smiling on the inside."

"These clothes were in style. Honestly, they were!"

"I'm cooler than I look."

"Smile? Would you smile if you were with these people?"

And like them
Eat Dead Flies

Roll a magazine up (or use a flyswatter) and chase a fly around the room. When it lands, smash it. Then, make sure someone with a weak stomach is watching and pull it off the magazine and pop it in your mouth. Yum! **P.S.** If you want to cheat — like we did — put a raisin on the magazine before the whole scam starts.

1

2

3

4 SPLAT!

5

6 YUM!

7

8

The Dead Finger

You'll need an empty small box (matchbox-sized) plus a little bit of baby powder or flour. Add some red nail polish or ketchup and a cotton ball or two.

Punch a big hole in the bottom of the box and stick your finger through. Then (with someone's help) powder up your finger so it looks totally dead. Pack it with cotton and splash a little nail polish around.

Then, when everyone is getting ready for dinner, bring in the box, tell a huge whopper about finding this amazing thing, and then slowly uncover it.

The person is still attached to this finger.

Photocopy this page many times

Make Your Own Barf Bag

You wouldn't think that taping this little sign to your lunchbag would make the sandwich inside taste any different. But somehow… it does.

MOTION DISCOMFORT CONTAINER

PLEASE USE IN THE EVENT OF MOTION DISCOMFORT OR NAUSEA. HOLD TO MOUTH. REPEAT.

A little video trickery
Meet Owl Man

Another fine opportunity to misuse that video camera (even the kind in a cell phone).

If you have a friend who can actually turn his head all the way around, that would be the easiest method to shoot this little movie. If you don't, try this instead.

Get a friend to stand in front of the camera and smoothly swivel his head from shoulder to shoulder. Then freeze. Stop the camera.

Now get him to take off his shirt, jacket, etc. and put them on backwards. Your friend then goes back to the same position, but this time facing away from the camera. Get him to put his chin back on the same

shoulder and restart the camera as he swivels it back to the other shoulder. The goal is to make it look as if there are no jumps or edits, so everything has to be smooth and unjerky. Good luck. It can be done.

More video trickery

The Balducci Levitation

Doing this stunt in public takes a bit of gall since it is totally dependent on angles. If your audience gets suspicious and starts moving around, you're busted. To prevent that, do it in a hallway. Or another option: Do it for your friend who's holding a video cell phone. Then you control the angles.

Get your cameraman to stand about 10 feet away from you.

Turn so you're three-quarters facing the camera and shift your feet as shown. The heel farthest from the camera is visible, but the rest of that foot should be hidden by the near foot.

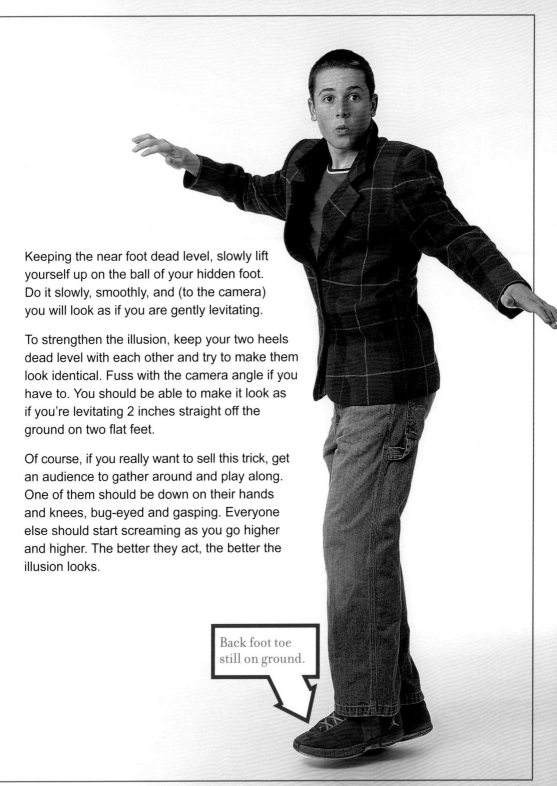

Keeping the near foot dead level, slowly lift yourself up on the ball of your hidden foot. Do it slowly, smoothly, and (to the camera) you will look as if you are gently levitating.

To strengthen the illusion, keep your two heels dead level with each other and try to make them look identical. Fuss with the camera angle if you have to. You should be able to make it look as if you're levitating 2 inches straight off the ground on two flat feet.

Of course, if you really want to sell this trick, get an audience to gather around and play along. One of them should be down on their hands and knees, bug-eyed and gasping. Everyone else should start screaming as you go higher and higher. The better they act, the better the illusion looks.

Back foot toe still on ground.

Do-It-Yourself Dog Barf

Here's an old family recipe of ours. It looks like vomit. But it tastes better. A little. It might be able to turn boys into frogs. We're not sure. We've never gotten one of them to eat it.

INGREDIENTS:

1/4 cup applesauce

1 packet of unflavored gelatin

plain instant oatmeal*

pinch of powdered chocolate

DIRECTIONS:

1. Heat applesauce in frying pan over low to medium heat.

2. Stir in unflavored gelatin.

3. Add a small pinch of powdered chocolate.

4. Mix thoroughly and remove from heat.

5. Sprinkle oatmeal over the mixture for looks.

6. Spray a plate with non-stick stuff (or put a little oil on it).

7. Spread the mess onto the plate.

8. Allow to cool.

*You can use other edible items like raisins, Raisin Bran® or spices for looks.

How to make
Frankentoys

Making Frankentoys is a wonderful art form that blends creative juices and destructive impulses. And while we can't really provide step-by-step instructions here for the simple reason that everybody has a different collection of old toys lying around, we can provide inspiration and a few basic tips for the beginning Frankentoy builder.

Don't plan, just build. Frankentoys are discovered, not invented.

Tape it. Glue, unless you want to use hot melt, usually isn't strong enough.

Name everything afterwards.

Susie Wiffles

Frisbee
Tinkerbottom

Little Miss
Quack Quack

Difficulty factor: Maximum

We Can't Figure This #*$!@ Puzzle Out!

This is an old puzzle, but it is way too hard for us. Once, some smart person told us how to do it, but we have forgotten. If you figure it out, please e-mail us the answer. Thank you.

Pretend you have a little teeter-totter as your scale. And you have six pool balls (two of them are red, two white, two blue).

FIRST WEIGHING:

Put some balls on the scale. Any number you like.

? ?

Your pretend teeter-totter

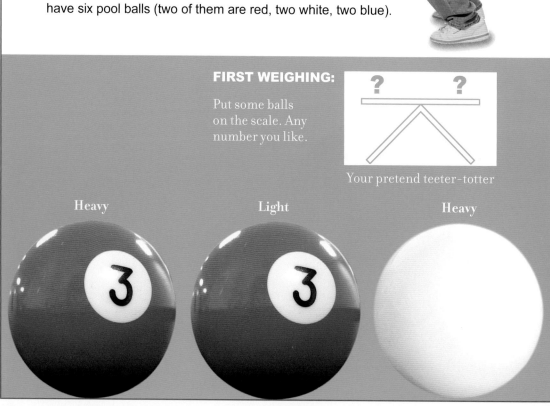

Heavy

Light

Heavy

In each color pair, one of the balls is light, and one of the balls is heavy. (So there's a heavy red and a light red, a heavy blue and a light blue, and a heavy white and a light white.)

All the light balls weigh the same, and all the heavy balls weigh the same. All the balls feel identical since the weight difference is small.

Your job (and we don't envy you) is to use the balance scale to figure out which are the heavies and which are the lights in every color pair. You can put any number of balls you like on either side of the scale. But you only get two separate weighings.

NOTE: This is a fair puzzle. No cheats and no tricks. Good luck.

Answer in back.

SECOND WEIGHING:

You can shuffle the same balls, or weigh new ones. Up to you. But if you do it right, you'll know which three balls are heavy, and which three balls are light after only two weighings.

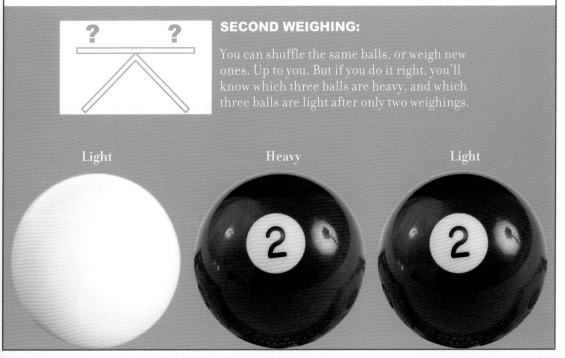

Light   Heavy   Light

Ping-Pong® Ball Burbling

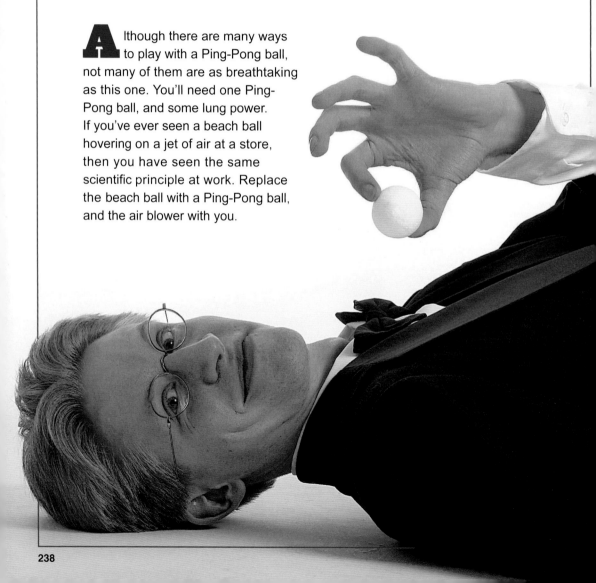

Although there are many ways to play with a Ping-Pong ball, not many of them are as breathtaking as this one. You'll need one Ping-Pong ball, and some lung power. If you've ever seen a beach ball hovering on a jet of air at a store, then you have seen the same scientific principle at work. Replace the beach ball with a Ping-Pong ball, and the air blower with you.

Place the ball carefully on your beautifully pursed lips. Then very, very, very slowly… begin blowing. If you filled your lungs with air, like we should have told you at the start, you might be able to get it to levitate like we did (on our fourth try).

For cheaters. Use a funnel. Blow through the narrow end.

Hovered for 3.1 seconds

Parental myths

Will Your Eyes Be Ruined by Reading in Bad Light?

In an effort to shed the bright light of truth as widely as possible, we are publishing the following scientifically checked information in an effort to foster greater honesty between the generations.

MYTH: Sugar causes tooth decay.

TRUTH? The truth is tooth decay is caused not by sugar but by bacteria pee. Bacteria pee is a nasty liquid that bacteria ooze when they're living and eating on your teeth. Of course, bacteria do especially well on sugar, so your parents aren't entirely wrong. But it always pays to be scientifically correct and that's all we're trying to do here.

MYTH: If you read in bad light, you will ruin your eyes.

TRUTH? Reading in poor light might tire your eyes, but it will do no damage. It's a bit like taking a picture in bad light. Doesn't make a very good picture, but it doesn't harm the camera. By the way, getting too close to the TV won't make you blind either.

MYTH: Chewing gum sticks to your heart if you swallow it. Or it takes seven years to digest.

TRUTH? If you swallow your gum, it will be dissolved and on its way to the sewage treatment plant within 48 hours.

MYTH: If you don't wash behind your ears, worms will grow there.

TRUTH? Ummmmm, no.

MYTH: Bundle up or you'll get a cold.

TRUTH? Wintertime is flu season because people are indoors more and sharing viruses.

MYTH: Sit up straight.

TRUTH? Sitting up straight is especially bad for your lower back. It compresses vertebrae, the bones of your spine. The healthiest posture for your back is reclining.

MYTH: Popping your knuckles will give you arthritis.

TRUTH? If you can create little bubbles in the fluid surrounding your knuckles, and then burst the bubbles by moving your joints a particular way, then you are a knuckle-popper. Fantastic skill and completely harmless.

MYTH: Carrots will improve your vision.

TRUTH? Not unless you are eating a vitamin-poor diet.

MYTH: You have to wait 30 minutes after you eat or you'll get cramps in the water.

TRUTH? Years ago the Red Cross used to publish this warning, but they have long since withdrawn it.

How to take
Pictures of Tiny People

The secret to this camera trick is the background. You want to find a simple background. It works bests when everyone can be positioned below the horizon line.

Big grassy hills work great. The photographer moves everyone into position (hand signals work well) until the effect looks right.

TIP: You want your hand as flat as possible so it looks like the tiny person is standing on your palm. The director directs everyone and moves the camera until it looks right.

Background distracting.
Hand not high enough.

WRONG! Palm is visible.

WRONG! Hand not touching.

RIGHT! Hand is flat.

Background better.

TIP: Position everybody so the background is not distracting.

KEY POINT: If your camera has this adjustment, set it on landscape (maximum shutter size). The important thing is to keep the foreground AND the background in focus.

Foreground and background in focus.

Foreground and background in focus. Can't see into bucket.

Put a Hole in Your Hand

Roll a piece of paper up into a tube and put it up to one of your eyes so you have a little porthole view of the world. Keep your other eye open normally. Then hold a hand up next to the tube, as shown. If you keep both eyes open, you'll get a weird view of your hand with a big hole in it.

How come?

It's another example of your brain putting one and one together. A little circular view of the world comes in from one eye. The other brings in a normal picture of a hand. Your brain adds the two together, as it does every second of every day, and gets a hole + hand.

Keep both eyes open and focus on something distant.

Camera fun time!

How to Be a Mutant

Here's a chance to get those big hairy legs you've always dreamed about. Find a willing hairy-legged grown-up who doesn't mind getting sat upon. Then, step two, sit on him. Put your legs kind of back out of the way and cover both the grown-up and your legs with a blanket or something. Bring in the audience or video camera and start in on a couple of hairy-legged jokes or stories.

Little Girl with Big Legs

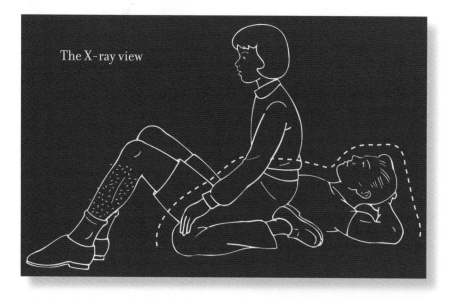

The X-ray view

Here's another terrific new way to re-model your whole appearance in a huge hurry. All you need is a willing partner who's wearing something like a loose sweatshirt or jacket, a pair of shoes and a blanket. Oh, yes — and a pair of boxers.

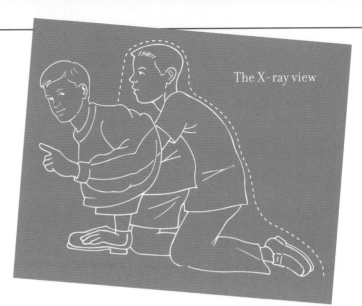

The X-ray view

1 Partner pulls arms out of sweatshirt.

2 You hunker down behind him, get yourself covered with the blanket and reach into partner's empty sweatshirt sleeves (this takes a little personal closeness).

3 Partner puts arms through boxers and into shoes. Maybe get a friend to tidy things up a bit, just to get the appearances correct, and you're all set. You'll look like The Munchkin from Mars. For a quick, cheap thrill, just holler for your parents to come into your room. They will freak out and then rush off for the camera.

Teenage Mutant Munchkin

How to Make a Dollar Bill Ring

This is a compelling project. Do not skip it, even if you normally don't like little crafty things. This one is different. You'll be working with real money (always exciting), and when you're finished you can parade around with an extremely eye-catching little ring — permanent, too — at least until that weak moment when you give in and spend it.

P.S. Don't worry about the instructions. They may seem long, but that's because we tend to be painfully clear. Nothing is assumed. Everything is illustrated. Just take it step-by-step. It's really not that bad.

1. Go get a nice, crisp one-dollar bill. An old limp bill is worthless. Don't even try.

2. Lay your bill on a tabletop with George right-side up and facing you. Fold the back bottom margin toward you and crease it down firmly. (Note I said back bottom margin. The back margins are a little bigger than the front. For this fold — and all the folds that follow — use a pencil or something to crease them well. And be precise. Neatness counts.)

Fold up.

3 Fold the top half down to cover the bottom, but don't bring it down quite all the way. Leave it short of the bottom edge by just a hair. As always, finalize the crease well with a pencil.

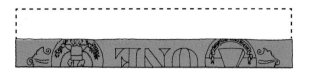

4 Now fold the top half down again. This time, though, bring it perfectly to the edge.

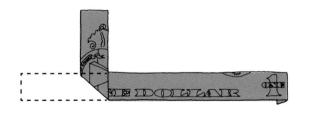

5 Turn the bill over and fold the right margin under.

6 Now fold the left side up exactly as illustrated. The "N" in ONE should be exactly half-visible when you're done.

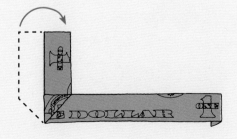

7 Next, flip the vertical part over, as shown. Crease well.

8 Turn the bill over, hold it in your hand exactly as shown…

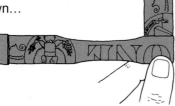

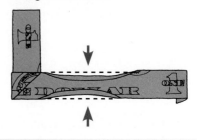

Optional Step

Fold top and bottom like this, in curves, if you like the graceful look.

…then wrap it around the tip of your left forefinger. When you're done, pinch it with your thumb.

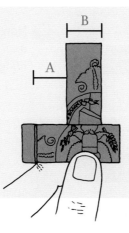

B

A

Key Point:
The dimensions "A" and "B" have to be the same.

9 Switch hands and hold the bill as shown.

10 Now, fold down the vertical part of the bill. (Lift up your thumb in order to do this and put it back down when you're done.)

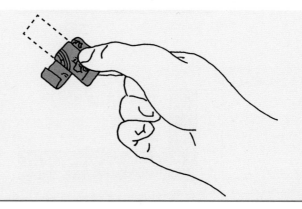

Bent-over tab

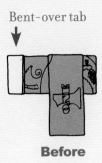

Before

11 Next, fold the **1** part across the front of the ring. Lift your thumb as you do this, and put it back down when you finish. (If the **1** isn't centered, you've been a little sloppy. Back up a few steps and adjust.)

Bent-over tab

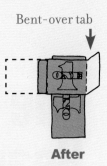

After

Bent-over tab tucked in under the **1**.

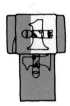

12 Tuck the bent-over tab (we colored it yellow) under the **1**.

13 Turn the ring over and find the diagonal slot. Tuck the part we marked in purple into the diagonal slot.

Diagonal slot

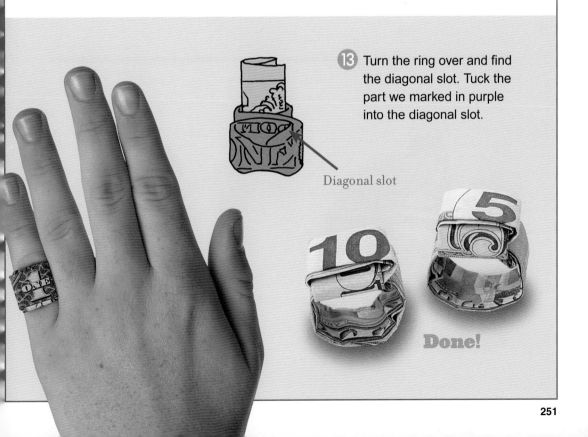

Done!

The Study Hall Head Bonk

Imagine the following picture: You're hard at work in the study hall or classroom, when suddenly your head slips off your hand and you bonk it against the desk, making a sound like an ax chopping wood. Naturally, you get up from your desk and stagger around holding your aching head. If you play it right, the teacher lets you go to the nurse's office.

Check out the photos below and you can make this fantasy real.

Watch the bottom hand.

KEY POINT:
Fake the head bonk. All the noise comes from under the table where you rapped it with your hand.

③

④

How to Stick a Pencil in Your Ear

Backstage View

Slide pencil through hand.

How to take it back out of your nose

The hand moves… not the pencil.

After you learn this one, you'll find yourself wondering how you ever got along without it. It's that useful.

Although we used a pencil in these photographs, don't let that limit you. You can stick all sorts of things in your ear if you concentrate. If you're in the kitchen, try a carrot; if you're in a restaurant, try a fork or spoon.

Backstage View

Slide hand down pencil.

Note: Eraser is touching jacket.

The Coat Hanger and the Quarter

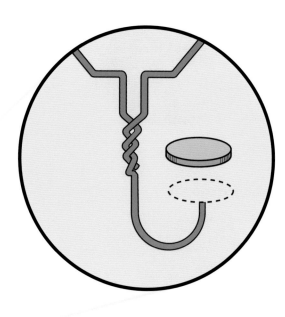

This is one of the hardest shenanigans in this book. It can be done, but it takes faith, patience, coordination, courage and a quarter. Don't go into this one expecting instant gratification. It may take ten minutes, it may take a day, but it's worth whatever you have to put into it. The end result is incredible. You will balance a quarter on the end of a hanger and spin the hanger around your finger. The quarter never moves.

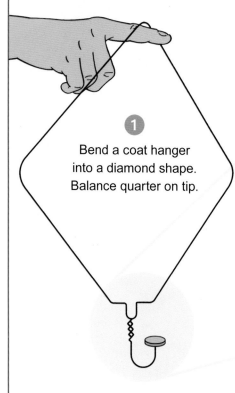

①

Bend a coat hanger into a diamond shape. Balance quarter on tip.

WARNING:
There is an excellent chance that you will send a coat hanger flying during this activity, so clear out the area first!

2 Coin balanced on tip. Hanger on finger.

3 Begin to rock the hanger back and forth.

4 Go for the full circle. For at least an hour you will fail to do it.

One hour later

5 Bring to a gentle stop by making a big "9." Use your knees and arm. Quarter still in place.

Photocopy this page!

The Peanut Butter Booger Hunt

Fill to line.

You will need some peanut butter and an empty half-pint or pint milk container. Half-fill the container with peanut butter, tape the new picture over the container, and poke two holes (dotted circles) with a pencil. Now whenever you want peanut butter, just stick your finger in and root around.

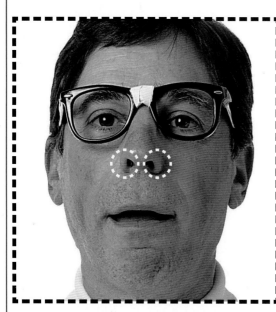

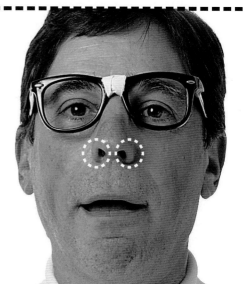

Make Your Friends Wonder Why They Put Up with You

1 Pull a quarter out of your pocket the next time you and your friend are sitting down somewhere.

2 Close your eyes and roll it up and down your face, forehead to chin. Make low moaning noises, like you do when something feels really good.

3 When your friend asks to try, pull out another quarter, the one you've doctored up by smearing pencil lead all over the edge, and give it to them. When they roll it up and down their face, two things will happen. First, they'll discover it doesn't feel particularly good at all, and second, they'll leave a big pencil line up and down their face. **Hysterical.**

How Much Salt Do You Take in Your Coffee?

This trick was dated when the ancient Greeks wrote it up, so it's hard to call it fresh and brand new. But you just can't write about immaturity without including it, so here it is, a true classic.

Unscrew the cap to a sugar dispenser and place a paper napkin over the opening. Shake a little salt onto the napkin.

Screw the cap back on over the napkin. Tear off the excess so no one can see the napkin is in there.

Stand back and watch the fun!

1 Start like this.

2 Cover the sugar dispenser with a napkin.

3 Put in the salt.

4 Screw on the lid.

5 Tear off the napkin that shows.

6 Your work here is done.

The Sleeping Parent
and the Shaving Cream

1 Locate sleeping adult.

2 Squirt a dab of shaving cream (or toothpaste) in his or her hand.

This activity is old enough to be the subject of a cave drawing. A true classic. The steps are quite simple, but the effect is timelessly entertaining.

3 Tickle nose with thread.

4 **Hide!**

Do Any of Your Friends Trust You?

If any of your friends still trust you, ask them this question and that should cure them.

Quarter Snatching

This is one of those tricks that everyone's favorite uncle can do — or at least he should. Load up your arm with quarters — one if you're a rank beginner, four if you've got mad skills. Then swoop your hand down and catch them all mid-air. Speed and confidence — that's all it takes.

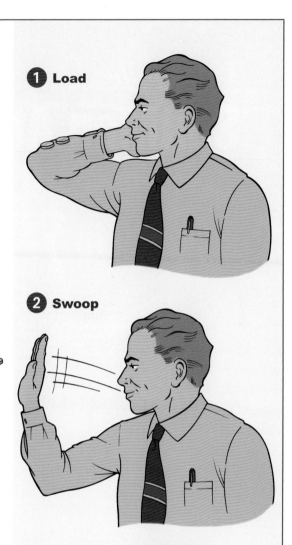

1 Load

2 Swoop

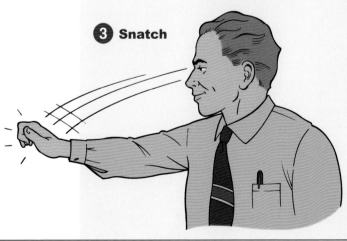

3 Snatch

Video follies!

SpitMan Attacks!

If you've got a video camera (even the kind that comes in cell phones or digital still cameras), you have a powerful tool for immaturity at your command. Here are a few ideas to get you started.

DogCam. Walk around the house holding the camera at your shin while making suitable growling and barking noises. Bump into a cat, or find a hydrant, for extra realism.

SpitMan Attacks!
The secret is the hose.

Handmade Bubbles

The next time you're standing in front of a sinkful of soapy water, being a little angel and washing the dishes like you always do, try this little bubbly trick.

Pretend your hands are like sliding doors. Start with the "doors" closed and in the water. Take them out of the water and slowly slide them open while you blow from about a foot away.

By the way, we've done a lot of work in this area. The absolute best bubble juice in the world is made from the following recipe.

12 cups water
1 cup Ultra Joy®
1 cup cornstarch
2 Tbsp. baking powder (not baking soda)

Rattlesnake Eggs

Imagine their thrill when they open it and it jumps out of their hands, rattling like crazy!

Imagine a friend or family member of yours finding a mysteriously sealed envelope on the table marked:

Danger!
Rattlesnake eggs.
Keep Refrigerated!
DO NOT OPEN!

How to do it

You'll need a sheet of good cardboard, a good rubber band and an envelope.

1 Cut the cardboard into two pieces using the stencils on the next page. One piece looks like a handle; the other piece is the flapper.

2 Cut the rubber band and thread it through the flapper. Thread and knot the rubber band onto the handle. Follow the pictures. Wind the band up tightly and keep it wound while you slide it into a letter-sized envelope.

3 Write the warning on the outside of the envelope.

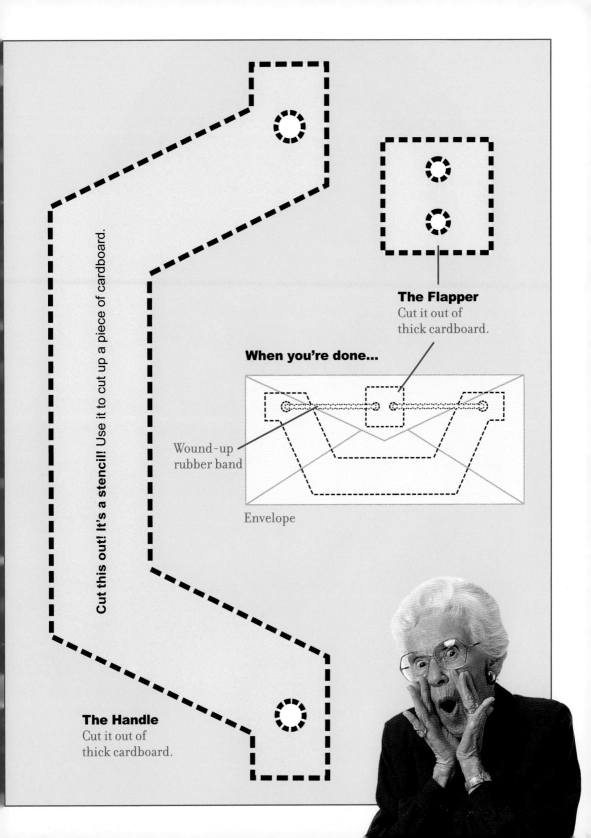

Cut this out! **It's a stencil!** Use it to cut up a piece of cardboard.

The Flapper
Cut it out of
thick cardboard.

When you're done...

Wound-up
rubber band

Envelope

The Handle
Cut it out of
thick cardboard.

Cut out.

Cut this out! It's a stencil! Use it to cut up a piece of cardboard.

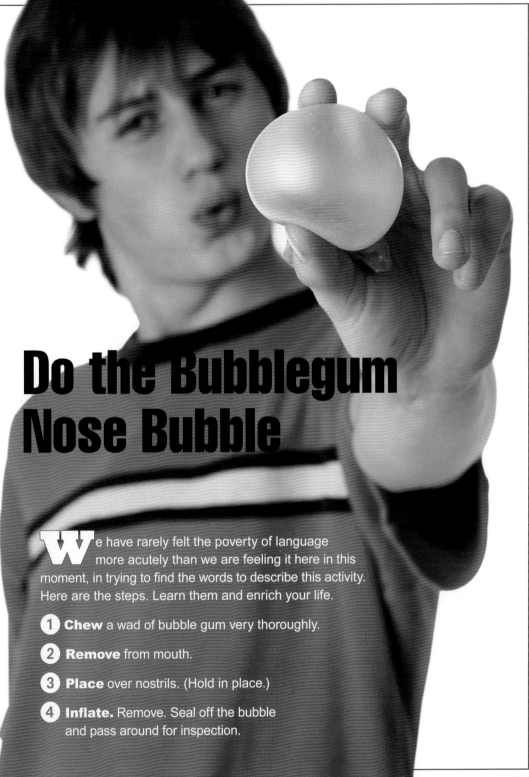

Do the Bubblegum Nose Bubble

We have rarely felt the poverty of language more acutely than we are feeling it here in this moment, in trying to find the words to describe this activity. Here are the steps. Learn them and enrich your life.

1. **Chew** a wad of bubble gum very thoroughly.

2. **Remove** from mouth.

3. **Place** over nostrils. (Hold in place.)

4. **Inflate.** Remove. Seal off the bubble and pass around for inspection.

Hello? Get Me Elbow on the Line!

The guy who showed us this prank claims that the Three Stooges rejected it for being too dumb. Sounded good to us.

Here's how it goes:

Ask a good friend to put out a fist.

Cover it with your other hand flat like this.

Your friend →

You

The rest is easy. Lean over, pick up his hand, put it to your ear like a telephone and say:

Grab My Thumb...
Gee, You're Dumb

Here's a bit of hand jive that scores very poorly on the maturity scale. Which is why we're including it. It's an extension of your basic high five.

Follow these steps:

1 Go fist to fist.

> **Gimme five!**

2 Switch hands.

> **Other side.**

...and do it again.

3 Hold elbow up and make your friend do the same. Bonk elbows.

> **Give me a 'bow.**

Smash a Grape Through Your Head

"Follow me and do everything exactly the way I do it!"

1 Before anyone's watching, put grape in mouth. Do NOT swallow.

Grape

Do this secretly!

2 Put another grape in your hand. Pinch its stem between your fingers.

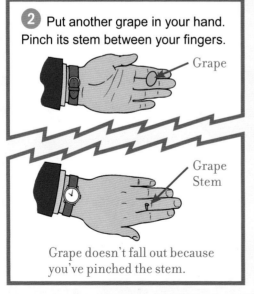

Grape

Grape Stem

Grape doesn't fall out because you've pinched the stem.

3 FAKE THIS PART!

Grape stays here because it's pinched.

Dump the grape from one hand to the other. Only don't really do it. Just make it look good.

4 Then smash grape against forehead.

Whoops! Check that!
Slap your forehead with the hand that <u>doesn't</u> have the grape. The grape is in your <u>other</u> hand.

Grape

THE FINALE

After you've smashed it, spit it out of your mouth! (Actually, spit the grape out of your mouth that you put there before the whole thing started and before anyone was watching.)

Chinnikins and the Attack of the Potbellied Pillow People

You'll need to lie down on a bed and hang your head over the edge. Put a T-shirt over your head and get someone to draw (with skin-safe markers) a face on your chin. Once again, turn up the music but this time lip-synch your way through the song.

Two words: Oh, baby.

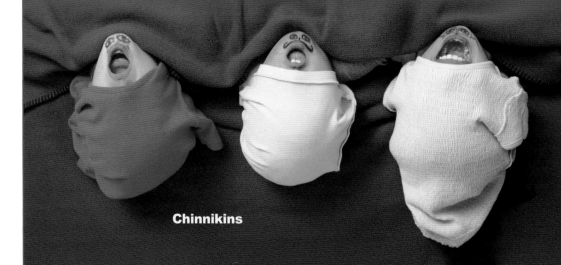

Chinnikins

Potbellied Pillow People

Wrap a puffy jacket around your waist and zip it up. Sleeves into the pockets. Then, get someone to put a pillowcase over your head and torso. Turn the music up loud and dance appropriately.

After watching a slumber party performance of the chinnikins and potbellied pillow people, your life will be changed forever. There is nothing on stage or screen that can possibly prepare you for this. This is why they invented video cameras.

Cinch jacket around waist.

Your parents never told you

Facts About Vegetables

If you spread your peas out, it will look like you ate more. If you are down to a single piece of broccoli, try sticking it in your milk. An upside-down sweet potato, if it's been flattened, can look as if it's been eaten. Technically, tomatoes are not vegetables (they're fruit). So the instruction "Eat your vegetables" does not apply to tomatoes.

Is candy corn a vegetable? You be the judge.

Eating beets can cause "beeteria," a condition in which your pee turns red.

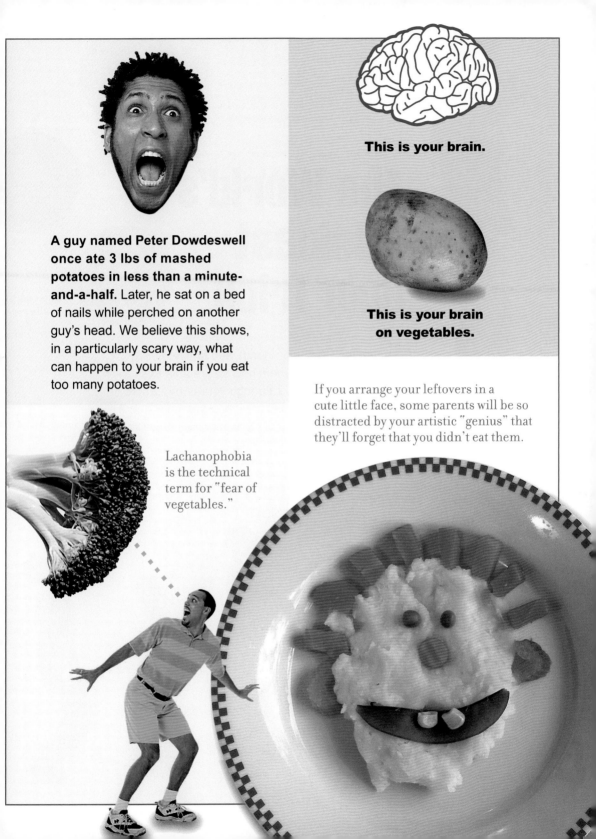

A guy named Peter Dowdeswell once ate 3 lbs of mashed potatoes in less than a minute-and-a-half. Later, he sat on a bed of nails while perched on another guy's head. We believe this shows, in a particularly scary way, what can happen to your brain if you eat too many potatoes.

This is your brain.

This is your brain on vegetables.

If you arrange your leftovers in a cute little face, some parents will be so distracted by your artistic "genius" that they'll forget that you didn't eat them.

Lachanophobia is the technical term for "fear of vegetables."

The World's Stinkiest Coin Trick

Imagine what your friends and family will say when you show them how you're able to swallow a coin, instantly pass it through your body's entire digestive system, collect it on the other end — and then allow them to inspect it as much as they like!

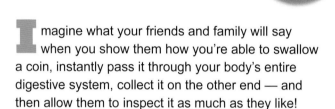

Check out my cool quarter.

Fake toss it in the air.

Fake swallow it.

1. Reach into your pocket and pull out a quarter. Show everyone. Then, with your other hand, take it and announce, "If I were to swallow this coin, it would really hurt… twice."

2. Then toss it up high in the air, catch it in your mouth and swallow it.

NO WAIT! This is a trick! You have to fake this stuff. Get the coin out of your pocket, but after that, fake it all — the toss and the swallow. While the coin is "making" its way through your body, make a bunch of weird faces. Then, reach around behind yourself (with the hand that still has the coin) and "collect" it from back there.

"Ta-Da!"

Sniff it once or twice and make a gross face. "Yup. It's the real thing." Then pass it around for inspection.

Fake digest it.

Fake this part, too.

Wanna inspect it?

The quarter is still in your hand because you never tossed it. Remember?

Spin a Wicked Curve Pen

F ind a ballpoint pen whose guts you can pull out. When you're done it should be a hollow plastic tube like this.

How to do it

On a cleared-off table, place the pen as shown and put your fingertips in place. Get ready to press REALLY hard so the pen squirts out from under your fingers and skitters down the table. It's a bit tricky, like learning how to snap your fingers, but you're on the right track if it kind of hurts every time you do it. The goal is to give enough spin to the tube that it doesn't just scoot down the table. You want to make it climb into the air and fly away. The trick is all in the spin. Good luck.

When it squirts out it should be back-spinning fast.

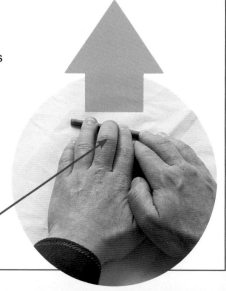

Press really hard. Add a lot of backspin.

Tricky stickies

Cream of Sock Soup

Tricky stickies are an easy and valuable way to redecorate the cans and boxes in your fridge or food cupboard. All you need are scissors and a glue stick. Or, if you're really persnickety, you could tear this page out and photocopy it onto sticker paper. Up to you. Just know that whichever you do, you'll be working with the best trickies in the business.

How to Be a Backseat Annoyance

Siren Sounds

With mouth closed, make a noise like a siren. Huge bonus if the driver believes you and pulls over. (It IS possible!)

Line Fights

When parent draws imaginary line between you and seatmate, push whatever stuff you have over it and say, "I am NOT over the line!"

Fake Fights

Clap your hands together and then holler "He HIT me!" Then fake cry. Huge bonus if driver believes you and hollers at seatmate.

Get Around the "Don't Touch Him!" Rule

After fighting with seatmate, and after receiving the "DON'T-EVEN-TOUCH-HIM" warning, point your forefinger at his cheek from about one millimeter away and say, "I'm not touching you!"

Repeat.

What's a "Puzzla"?

It's a paragraph such as this. It's not at all normal, but why? Only you will know (assuming you look in the back). Hand it out to any of your pals… and no hints.

Note to user:

Give the paragraph below to anyone who needs something to do with their brain for awhile. Its trick is obvious to those who know, but quite opaque to those who don't.

How quickly can you find out what is unusual about this paragraph? It looks so ordinary that you would think that nothing was wrong with it at all; and in fact, nothing is. But it is unusual. Why? If you study it and think about it you may find out, but I am not going to assist you in any way. You must do it without coaching. No doubt if you work at it for long, it will dawn on you. I don't know. Now, go to work and try your luck.

The complete rules

How to Play SHOTGUN!

The basic rule.
If you are the first to see the car and holler "Shotgun!" you may walk slowly to the car, smug in the knowledge that your seat in the front is reserved. It doesn't matter if you are not actually first to arrive at the car. **What matters is who hollers first, not who gets to the car first!**

- **You must be able to see** the car before you can holler "Shotgun!"

- **If no one hollers** "Shotgun!" and you get your hand on the door handle, you are awarded shotgun automatically.

- **No pre-hollering.** In other words, the errand has to be over and you have to be on your way back to the car before you holler "Shotgun!" Example: You and a sib are getting out of the car on the way to a store. You cannot holler "Shotgun for on the way back!" This is laughable. A corollary: Knowing that the car is parked behind the big black truck, or around the next corner, is NOT the same as actually seeing it.

- **Window sightings.** Illegal. You cannot "see" the car through a window and holler. You must be outside in view of the car.

If you leave shotgun briefly (a gas station stop, for example) you still have shotgun rights but the clock starts ticking. You have 5 minutes. After that, the position is open. Other riders wishing to claim shotgun must holler, as usual, from outside the car.

How to Sneak Around

M ost kids think they already know how to sneak around. They think all you have to do is tiptoe around and hide behind the door and stuff like that.

How wrong they are.

It turns out there's a whole science to sneaking around. If you want to be a spy or detective, they teach courses in the spy and detective schools. We actually ordered the textbooks and boiled the information down to the essentials. Here they are: **11 key points for the truly sneaky**, whether outside or in.

1 **The Prime Rule:** Always act as if someone is actively looking for you at every moment. Whether you're inside or out, never relax and ALWAYS be ready to freeze.

2 **Inside:** If you can, walk next to the wall where the floor is less likely to squeak, especially in hallways. Support a lot of your weight on the handrail if you're on the stairs for the same no-squeak reason.

Stairs are less squeaky on the edge.

Under the desk. Key point: Don't move!

③ Inside: Move quickly when you're in the open and rest in complete silence (for 60 seconds or more) when you're safe. If someone hears a suspicious noise, they will pause and wait to hear additional sound. If you don't move for a long minute, they'll usually relax and think they were hearing things.

④ Inside: Always take advantage of covering noise. When your target is making noise, when a car is driving by, when people are talking — *that* is the time to move. It's *very* risky to move otherwise. Don't do it unless you have absolutely no choice. And remember: Even if you think they're too far away to hear you, always assume they can and always assume they're listening for you.

⑤ Inside your own house: Know where the floor-squeaks are and avoid them. Know which doors never get closed and be ready to duck behind them. Know the best hiding place in every room. Getting under the bed is an excellent choice since grown-ups hate getting down on their knees to look. If a bedspread is all rumpled up all the time anyway, think about jumping onto the bed and covering yourself with the bedspread. In the bathroom, you can step into the tub and pull the shower curtain out just enough to hide you.

Under a messy bedspread

Behind the shower curtain

6 **Inside:** If you're in a room with an open door, avoid the wall opposite it. That way, a quick glance won't get you. If you hear someone walking down the hall, freeze and squat down by a wall or beside or behind the furniture. You'd be amazed what you can get away with SO LONG AS YOU'RE NOT MOVING!

7 **Inside:** Any time you are higher or lower than eye level you're harder to see — which is why squatting down is so incredibly effective. If you can shinny up into a closet, they'll never find you. If you're hiding behind a door, squat down and leave the door halfway open. You'll hear people coming much better and a half-open door is less suspicious anyway.

Wear dark clothing.

8 **Outside:** The big no-no's are the same outside as in: noise and movement. Be ready to freeze at every instant. If you watch a cat hunting, it spends a tremendous amount of time stock-still.

9 **Outside:** Always be aware of your background. The worst is the sky or grass. The best is mixed shadow and light, buildings or trees. Stay low as much as possible. Stoop, crawl or if you have to, slither. Avoid wide-open spaces like the plague. If you have to get to the other side, make big semi-circular detours.

10 **Outside:** Use every possible bit of cover and when you're forced into the open, move quickly with covering noise. If you need to look around a tree or rock, do it very low and use only a single eye so the outline of your whole head doesn't show and make you more obvious.

11 **Outside:** If you're trailing someone on a street, never walk on the same side. Use crowds for cover. Walk beside strangers to make it seem as if the two of you are walking together since pairs are less suspicious. By the way, two people *can* trail one person much more effectively than one but only by splitting up and "handing the target off." In other words, take turns.

DO stay below the horizon.

DON'T allow yourself to be seen against the horizon.

The Top Ten Facts of All Time

Our readers often look to us for the answers to questions that ordinary scientists and learned men and women are either unable, or unwilling, to answer. Over the years, thousands of these probing, difficult questions have come to us. For the purposes of this encyclopedia, we have decided to list the top ten, in descending order. These are the questions that we believe are the most important. If you aspire to true immaturity, you need to know their answers. And by the way, we are not making any of this up.

Q. Where is Uranus?

A. We can't believe people keep asking us this one since the answer is so obvious. "Well, where do you think?" If the entire solar system were reduced to the scale of your body — with the sun at your head and Pluto at your feet — then Uranus would be located exactly where you think it'd be. Incidentally, if anyone ever asks you if Uranus has any rings around it, you should stand up and proudly say, "Yes, indeed! Nine, to be exact. But you can't see them with the naked eye. They are only visible through high-powered telescopes."

Q. Do mummies have brains?

A. We've been asked this question so many times that we finally went out and learned the real answer, which is something we ordinarily hate to do. It turns out that mummies don't have brains for the simple reason that the Egyptians dug them out and tossed them. They reached in through their mummy noses with little hooks and fished them out. It's all part of the mummification process. (There now, aren't you glad you asked?)

Doh.

Q. Do termites have gas problems?

A. Yes, they do. But before you act all surprised and grossed out, remember that termites eat wood and wood is difficult to digest. Try it sometime. The result is unfortunate, but hardly unexpected, often leading to awkward social situations. Incidentally, there are enough termites in the world, and each of them emits enough methane, that they (and cows, too, for that matter) have been identified as significant sources of greenhouse gases and thus, contribute to global warming. **P.S.** Ancient termites have been discovered trapped in pieces of amber in which tiny bubbles can sometimes be seen in a little chain coming from their south ends. How embarrassing is that?

Q. Are Martians dangerous?

A. Only one person that we know of has been killed by a Martian and there's an asterisk attached since the person was actually a dog (in Nakhla, Egypt, 1911). And the Martian was actually just a rock that came from Mars. But still. The rock was exploded off the surface of Mars millions of years ago by an asteroid impact. It then proceeded on a long flight plan that eventually ended on the head of an Egyptian dog. The meteorite was saved and, more than 50 years later, analyzed. Only then was it discovered to have originated on Mars.

Q. How do they get rid of all of the bugs before they make cereal and bread and stuff?

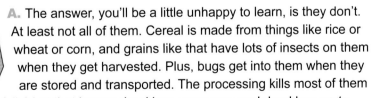

A. The answer, you'll be a little unhappy to learn, is they don't. At least not all of them. Cereal is made from things like rice or wheat or corn, and grains like that have lots of insects on them when they get harvested. Plus, bugs get into them when they are stored and transported. The processing kills most of them (hopefully) but that leaves dead bug carcasses and dead bug parts. Yuck. The law allows a percentage of every box of cereal to be "insect parts and bodies." Although you will not find them on the list of ingredients, they are in there. In two cups of cereal (50 grams) there are allowed to be 75 insect parts.

Q. I think my little brother is an ape. He says he's not. Who's right?

A. Technically speaking, he is; but it's actually very close. Ninety-nine percent of an ape's DNA is identical to human DNA.

Q. Are bugs bugged by bugs?

A. You'd think bugs would be nice to each other, since they're all about the same size and sort of look alike and so forth. But in fact, a lot of bugs are horrible to each other — really horrible. For example: Did you know that fleas have fleas? (We're calling them fleas, but they're actually mites.) Except that when you're already a flea, your own fleas are about the size of Frisbees (relatively speaking). Or think what life is like for the caterpillar. One species of wasp lays its eggs inside a caterpillar with its stinger. Then the baby wasp grows up, eating the caterpillar from the inside out. Yuck! Fortunately, caterpillars know how to fight dirty, too. They are able to eject their tiny doo-doo at high speed toward the attacking wasps. Ready! Aim! Fire doo-doo!

Flea with mites

Q. What do well-bred ladies do with whale vomit?
❑ Make weird faces and run away screaming.
❑ Use it as a condiment to spread on toast.
❑ Put it behind their ears.
❑ Mix it with salt and water and take for constipation.

A. The answer, you'll be pleased to know, is (3) put it behind their ears. But wait a minute! Don't worry! They don't use new whale vomit (that would be disgusting). They use old whale vomit. It washes up on beaches sometimes. French perfume manufacturers have used it for years in their more expensive fragrances. These days, good quality whale vomit is very rare and illegal to sell in the U.S. (Google "ambergris" if you don't believe us.)

Q. If the rate of population growth doesn't change in the future, what's going to happen?

A. The population of the Earth, which is a little over 6 billion people, will double every 40 years. Therefore, if we do the math, 2,400 years from now Planet Earth will be a packed ball of human flesh expanding outward at the speed of light.

Q. What would happen if a penny dropped off the Empire State Building and hit me on the head?

A. You'll probably be disappointed with this answer, but it would not burn a hole in your head. A falling penny acts a good bit more like a feather than a rock. A penny reaches a top speed of something like 40 mph in free fall. It might sting, but that's about it.

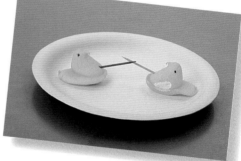

En garde!

Feel the sting of my toothpick.

And Peeps® jousting, too

Marshmallow Death Matches

Placing two marshmallows on a plate in a microwave for a fight to the death is an old kitchen sport as are Easter Peep jousting and pancake art.

Here is how it goes:

1 Stick a couple of toothpicks through two marshmallows.

2 Put them on a paper plate with their toothpicks pointing towards one another. Place your bets and place in microwave.

3 Turn it on (the microwave) and watch the death match through the window. It's all over in 15 seconds.

Before

After

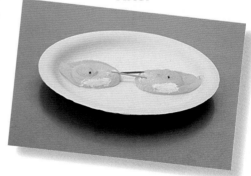

P.P.S. A chunk of Ivory® soap does an interesting mutational thing in a microwave, too. It's just that you can't eat Ivory soap afterwards.

P.S. You can use marshmallow Peeps if it's that time of year. Some people like the additional realism of that.

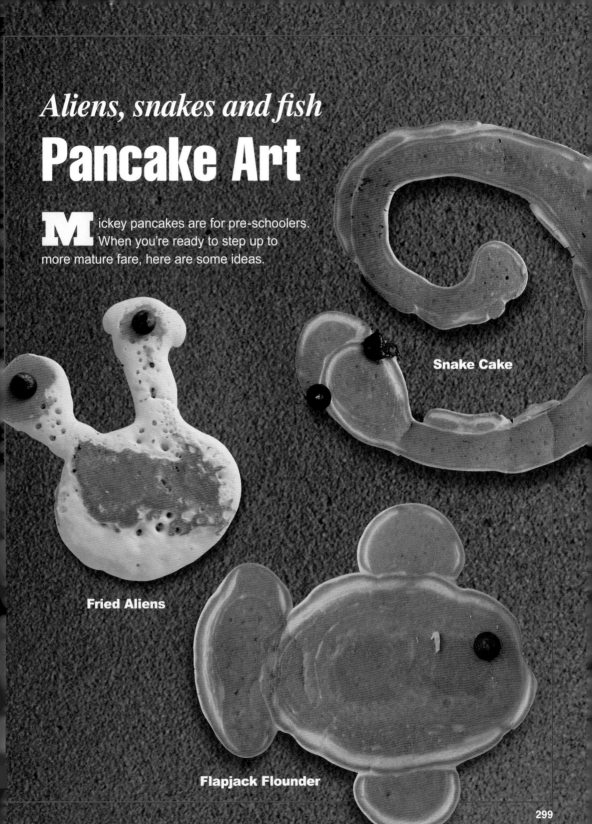

Aliens, snakes and fish

Pancake Art

Mickey pancakes are for pre-schoolers. When you're ready to step up to more mature fare, here are some ideas.

Snake Cake

Fried Aliens

Flapjack Flounder

Homemade Special FX

A video camera (even the kind that comes in cell phones or digital cameras) can be a dangerous tool for foolishness if it falls into the wrong hands. Here are a few ways to make sure your hands are wrong.

The See-Through TV. Shoot a blank wall for a few moments — the one that is behind the TV — and then put your head into the shot by slowly standing up in front of the camera. Smile. Then slowly drop back out. When you put the movie on the TV screen, get behind the TV and slowly stand up behind it when your "video head" makes its appearance. Then drop back out when your time on screen is up. This might take a little practice to get your timing right, but greatness like this is so worth it.

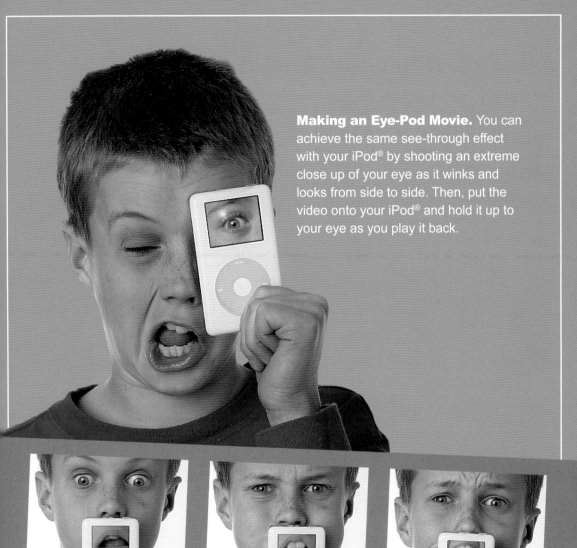

Making an Eye-Pod Movie. You can achieve the same see-through effect with your iPod® by shooting an extreme close up of your eye as it winks and looks from side to side. Then, put the video onto your iPod® and hold it up to your eye as you play it back.

Watch Your Mouth! Shoot an extreme close-up of your mouth lip-synching your favorite old song. Then put it onto your iPod® and hold it over your mouth while you play the song. It's a portable karaoke machine.

More how to play with your food
Sandwich Faces

It's amazing the people you can meet in a sandwich.

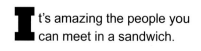
Peanut butter and scary

An MFT (Makin' Faces & Tomato)

What am I? Chopped liver?

①

**Take a
deep breath...**

How to Inflate Your Head

We usually do this one standing against a wall with a baseball cap on backwards. The instructions? Inhale, blow into thumb and lean back. Makes a nice video, too.

②

...and blow.

How to Give Sink Showers

We usually avoid the kind of pranks that leave the victim permanently maimed, emotionally scarred or soaking wet and fuming.

Usually.

1. Put rubber bands around the squirt handle thing that is on your sink. If you don't have a squirt handle thing on your sink, you shouldn't be reading this item, sorry.

2. Point the squirt handle thing at the place where someone's face is when they turn the water on.

3. Wait.

The Official Rules to Jinx

A great deal of confusion has grown up around Jinx because everybody seems to think they can make up their own rules. Obviously, this is a recipe for anarchy. As a result, we are publishing the official, no-more-arguments-ever-again international rules. We know they are official, because we wrote them. Please discard your own inaccurate, unofficial rules and use ours from here on in. Thank you.

When two people say exactly the same thing, at exactly the same time…

1 One person hollers "jinx" first. Let's say it's you. Immediately after you say "jinx" you should start counting as fast as possible to ten. When you get to ten, you get to say "Jinxed! You owe me a Coke®!"

2 The other person is now jinxed and cannot say anything until you say their name. The only way out of the jinx is to get you a Coke®.

3 **IMPORTANT EXCEPTION!** If the other person hollers "Jinx stop!" before you get to ten, you have failed to jinx them completely. If they holler "Jinx stop" while you were at the number five (for example), you are permitted to pinch them five times on the arm. But that's all. They can still talk.

TIP

In the morning, when the teacher is calling roll, get ready to pounce. When your victim's name is called, holler "here" right when they do and then go straight to the jinx. No matter what they say, there is nothing in the rules against this!

Immaturity 101

Have You Met My Sidekick?

This is really basic stuff and you probably already know it, but on the other hand, it's always good practice to review the fundamentals from time to time.

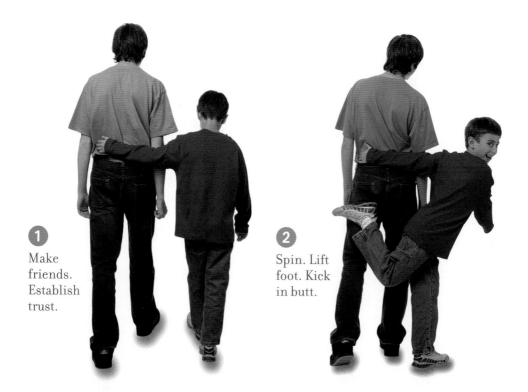

1 Make friends. Establish trust.

2 Spin. Lift foot. Kick in butt.

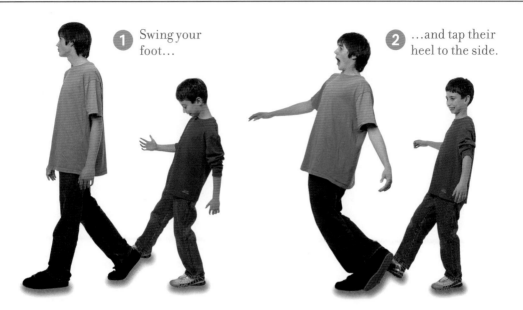

① Swing your foot…

② …and tap their heel to the side.

HEEL KICKING

Walk right behind someone and then tap their right heel to the left as they lift their foot. They'll kick themselves in the back of their own calf. Hysterical.

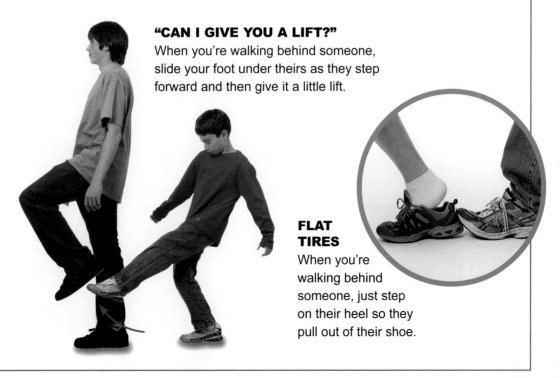

"CAN I GIVE YOU A LIFT?"

When you're walking behind someone, slide your foot under theirs as they step forward and then give it a little lift.

FLAT TIRES

When you're walking behind someone, just step on their heel so they pull out of their shoe.

You Could Put Your Eye Out with That

The magician Mac King is the creator of this small piece of genius, although this is a slightly modified version of the original. It's quite simple, but the effect can be life-altering (for your audience).

1 You'll need to be seated at a restaurant with a few of your closest friends. While no one is paying any attention to you, pick up the little container of cream stuff and pry the lid open just a tad or poke a hole in it. Conceal in your hand and make a fist. Don't let it leak. Yet.

Feels like something in my eye...

...something really sharp...

2 Begin complaining about something in your eye. Complain long enough, and loud enough, so that people finally start paying attention to you. When they do…

3 Bring your fist to your eye and begin rubbing.

4 Say "Owww. Feels like something really SHARP in my eye…!"

5 Rub harder and harder and finally squeeze and…

6

Eeeeeek!

Sub Day Shenanigans

Rarely in your life will an opportunity for immaturity raise its pretty head more attractively then on substitute days. There are thousands of ways to exploit this opportunity. We will list a few here, but obviously, the sky's the limit.

The Foreign Exchange Student Bit

If there's a kid in the class with a weird name — Sheboygan Vistalick or something — get everyone to whisper and explain to the sub: "He's the foreign exchange student from outer Antarctica.

"That's why he looks so blank.

"He doesn't speak English (make him grunt and do weird noises around here).

"And he becomes violent at the sound of the word 'homework' (get him to jump out of his desk and growl right here).

"In his language, it means something really bad."

Do you have any problem with our real teacher's award-winning progressive educational policies? Like no homework? And early dismissal?

The Boy Named Cheryl Bit

During roll, make some guy raise his hand and say "here" when the teacher gets to "Cheryl Lebowski" or some girl name like that. Then, when the sub looks up at the guy and says "Your name is Cheryl!?" he should put his head on his desk and start sobbing. Then everyone else can explain how sensitive Cheryl is about his name and a couple of other guys can help him to his feet and take him out to the nurse's office.

**Cheryl?
Are you all
right?**

More lame magic
The Floating Fork

Are you completely unreasonable? Do you want to be an incredible magician? But without spending any time on the boring practice part?

So do we!

Here's one trick that will help. You need to be at dinner with some friends.

1 Stick a knife into the tines of a fork and cover both with a napkin. Don't let anyone see you do this part.

2 Lift the napkin (and fork) as shown. Close your eyes and say a lot of things like *"boooga woooga wooo"* as you lift the fork (with your thumb) into and out of view.

Balance the Salt Shaker

If you're at a restaurant where they have those glass salt shakers, you can waste a good 5 minutes balancing it on one edge. Start by dumping a little pile of salt on the table. Then holler at everyone and make them pay attention to you and stop jiggling the table.

1 Balance on a little pile of salt.

2 Carefully blow the salt…

3 …away.

Pop an Apple Off Your Arm

This is one of those small skills that goes right up there with whistling and snapping your fingers. Hold the apple as shown, directly above your bent elbow. Drop it.

Wait a single heartbeat and then quickly straighten your arm (as if you were trying to punch someone right in the nose). The apple will hit the inside of your arm and pop up.

TIP:
Everybody wants to lift their arm to meet the falling apple. Not only is this unnecessary, it's counterproductive; it doesn't work. All you need to do is "drop... and punch." That's it.

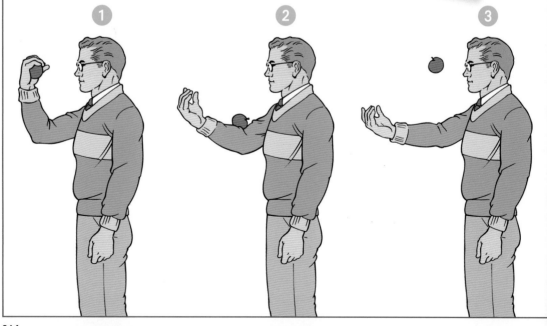

After

How to Be a Table

You'll need four people and four chairs. Arrange the four people exactly as shown. Everyone should put their head in their neighbor's lap. Then carefully pull all the chairs while everyone shifts around a bit to get their weight right.

Before

When everyone's settled, pull the chairs out.

Make a Fortune Teller

Any square piece of paper can be made into a Fortune Teller. But for truly spectacular results, we recommend you start with the pre-printed Fortune Teller on page 321.

1 Tear the pre-printed Fortune Teller out and place it face down. Cut on the dotted line.

Bring the two corners together exactly.

2 Fold two corners together and crease firmly.

3 Unfold. Then fold the other two corners together and crease again.

End up like this.
A square piece of
paper with two creases
running corner to corner.

4 Fold each corner point
into the center like this.

End up
like this.

Keep reading
• • • • • • • • • • • • ➤

5 Flip over. Then fold all four of the corners into the center. Do it carefully. Crease firmly.

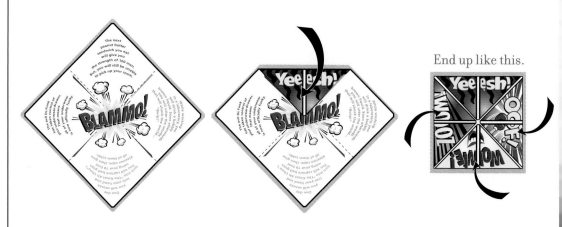

End up like this.

6 Fold it in half. This way.

7 Then unfold, and fold it in half the other way.

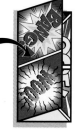

Done!

8 **The Big Finish**
Stick your thumbs and first two fingers into the four pockets on the bottom of the Fortune Teller.

How to Play

Get your player to choose one of the top four squares: Woo!, Bang!, Splat! or Crunch!

There are four words showing: **Woo!, Bang!, Splat!** and **Crunch!** Your player picks one, let's say **Woo!** That's a three-letter word, so you open and close three times. On the third opening make your player pick an inside flap.

Pick one of the four inside flaps.

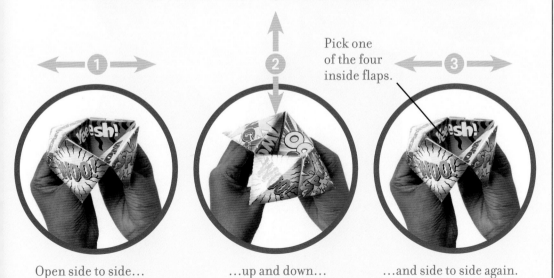

Open side to side...   ...up and down...   ...and side to side again.

The Moment of Truth

1 When he's picked one of the inside flaps…

2 Flip up the chosen panel.

3 Read the fortune under the panel.

You will have a bad hair day.

grrrr...

Every day.

How to Pop a French Fry

The cardboard container you get your French fries in makes a nice jack-in-the-box if you use it before it gets all greasy.

1 Grab the little cardboard container as shown.

2 Squeeze.

P.S. You've only got three or four pops before your container is popped out. So don't waste them.

Before

After

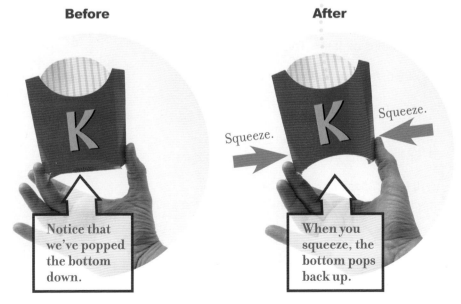

Squeeze.

Squeeze.

Notice that we've popped the bottom down.

When you squeeze, the bottom pops back up.

With a fortune teller

How to Play
Truth or Dare

① Tear out the next page and fold it up. Instructions on page 316.

② Stand in front of a dear friend and spin your Cootie Catcher until they say stop.

③ Open and close the Cootie Catcher as you spell their name.

④ When you're done spelling, your friend will be looking at four choices — truths or dares. They must pick one.

When they do, flip the panel and read it.

The KILLER BIG Rule:

If they choose **truth,** then become too shy to tell the truth, they MUST do the dare.

If they choose **dare,** then become too chicken to do the dare, they MUST tell the truth.

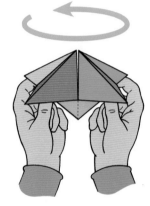

Spin the Fortune Teller around and around until your victim says stop. Then…

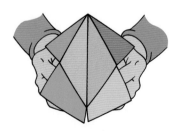

…open it and read.

truth

dare

Describe your dream date.

Suck on your thumb for the next minute.

dare

truth

Show us the Wubba Wubba dance.

What color is your underwear?

truth or dare

Free pass. Ask someone else a question.

Sing a short opera about what you did today.

truth

dare

dare

truth

Count to 10, like a duck.

If you could, what would you change about yourself?

How to Break Your Nose

How many times have you wanted to break your nose, but you just didn't know how?

Well, here are the easy-to-follow steps:

1 Put your hands over your nose like this. Make a horrible face and slowly, very slowly, bend your nose more and more until you hear a loud… POP!

2 Remove your hands and smile. You can get the all-important sound effects by either really breaking your nose (which we don't recommend) or secretly catching your thumbnail just under your front tooth and then, at just the right moment, popping it off as loud as you can.

Grab nose. Catch thumbnail under front tooth.

CRACK!

Slowly torque nose. Pop thumbnail off front tooth.

How to Spin a Pencil Around Your Thumb

Like most of the readers of this book, you probably finish all your tests early.

Of course, this creates a problem. What to do while all the other, less-gifted students struggle towards the bell?

One solution?

Learn how to spin a pencil! To learn it well can take an hour or more, but you can get the first few whiffs of success in 10 minutes. Put a jacket on your desk and practice above it so all the drops don't go to the floor.

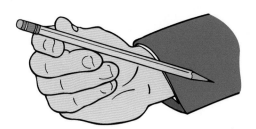

1 Starting position.

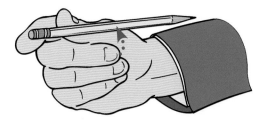

2 Kick the pencil with your middle finger.

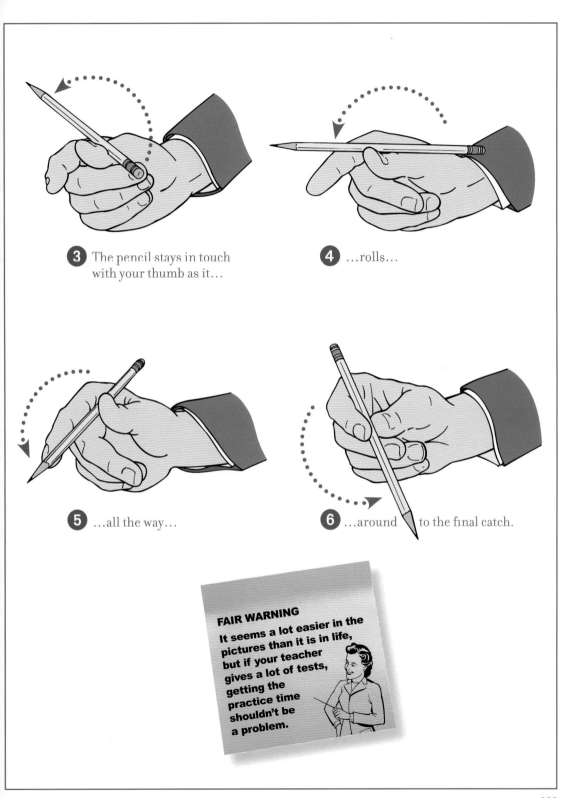

3 The pencil stays in touch with your thumb as it...

4 ...rolls...

5 ...all the way...

6 ...around to the final catch.

FAIR WARNING
It seems a lot easier in the pictures than it is in life, but if your teacher gives a lot of tests, getting the practice time shouldn't be a problem.

Starburst® papers work, too

How to Make a Chewing Gum Wrapper Chain

When you get famous, the people who write books about you will probably be interested in every detail about your life — like exactly how many pieces of chewing gum you chewed.

Plus, they'll be looking for things to put in museums. If you make a chain out of all the chewing gum wrappers you use, that'll help them in both ways.

Here are the instructions. Every time you chew a piece of chewing gum, save the wrapper and add a link to your chain. Do it for posterity.

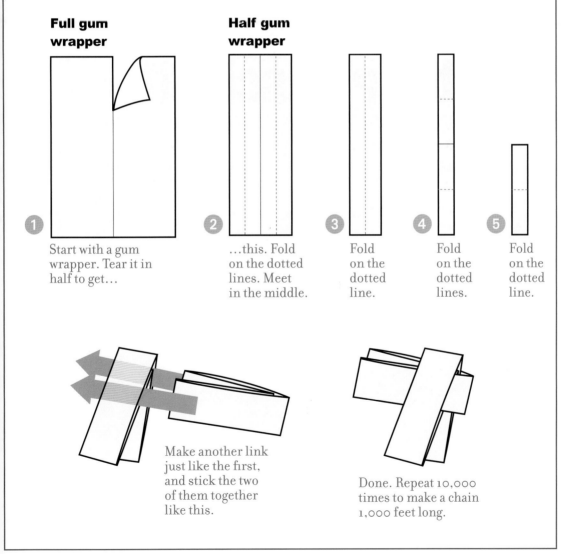

Full gum wrapper

Half gum wrapper

1 Start with a gum wrapper. Tear it in half to get…

2 …this. Fold on the dotted lines. Meet in the middle.

3 Fold on the dotted line.

4 Fold on the dotted lines.

5 Fold on the dotted line.

Make another link just like the first, and stick the two of them together like this.

Done. Repeat 10,000 times to make a chain 1,000 feet long.

The Wibble Wobble

Rubber Pencil Bit

Hold a pencil as shown (loosely) and wobble it up and down. It'll turn into rubber before your disbelieving eyes. (Or at least it'll look like it did.)

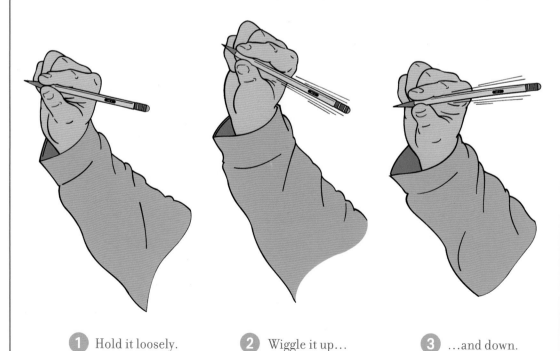

1 Hold it loosely.   **2** Wiggle it up…   **3** …and down.

How to Ride a Unicycle

For most people, riding a unicycle represents their last best chance of looking miraculous. Fortunately, it is an illusion. The miraculous part anyway. Although it is not 10-minute easy, it is no high-wire act. If you fuss around with it for a week, especially if you can find a corridor to practice in (touching two walls at once is the equivalent of unicycle training wheels), you'll get it.

Your unicycle should be as high as your belly button.

You'll probably have to buy your unicycle online. The big brands are Miyata® and Schwinn®.

Turn page.

Find a wall.
Or even better,
find a corridor.

GETTING UP ON YOUR BIKE

1

2

3

PRACTICE GETTING OFF YOUR UNI FORWARDS

1 Grab your seat as you…

2 …step off. Repeat. Get on your uni and then right off. Do it as often as you need to. Your goal is to relax.

PRACTICE GETTING OFF YOUR UNI BACKWARDS

Grab your seat, lean a little backwards, and pedal the uni forward. Hop off. You will survive.

The biggest fear in unicycling is falling backwards and cracking your skull. It's actually not easy to do. The reason is there's nothing to keep your feet in or hang you up. If you start to go over, hop off.

GETTING STARTED: HOW TO GO BACK... AND FORTH

Back up a half-turn.

Stop here.

Reverse direction for one half-turn.

Back vertical.

Seat leans back.

With your pedals at 12 and 6 o'clock, back up by pushing on your top pedal. Just a bit. Notice the seat stem leans back a tiny bit but your body stays vertical.

Back
vertical.

Seat
leans
forward.

Go
forward
a quarter
turn.

Stop
here.

End up
like this.

Now press on your bottom pedal and roll forward a little bit. Don't lean on the wall. Just use it for balance. You WILL have to hop off. Everybody does. Just get back up on that unicycle. You WILL learn.

Repeat. Go back and forth a few times.

DON'T
If you lean forward with your shoulders, the uni will shift forward and you'll fall off the back.

Bad back angle.

DO
If you lead with your hips, the uni will stay with you.

Roll this way…

ROLLING YOUR FIRST FEW FEET

Just touch the wall. Use it for balance, not for support.

Keep your weight off your feet. Sit on the unicycle and put your weight on the seat.

Go slow, but don't creep. Go forward a few feet. Stop. Back up. This may take a few hours, but you'll get there.

…and this way.

The Only Card Trick in This Book

Most decent card tricks take more practice than truly lazy people (like us) are willing to put in. However, there are a few exceptions (see one below). You'll need two identical decks of cards and a roll of tape. The effect goes like this:

1 Tape the EXTRA 2 of clubs someplace weird.

2 Welcome your victim.

2 of clubs is already on top of this deck.

Tape the extra 2 of clubs to the table.

5 Allow victim to see top card (the 2 of clubs).

6 Allow victim to cut the deck. Then stall. Put the halves back together exactly the way they came apart so that the 2 of clubs stays on top.

You shuffle a regular deck of cards a number of times.
Allow your audience to cut it. Then instruct them to pull
the top card and look at it without telling you what it is.
Then they will put it back into the deck anywhere they like.

You shuffle again and then suddenly heave the deck
against the wall where your stunned audience will find
their selected card mysteriously taped in place.

3 Demonstrate your
trustworthiness.

4 Shuffle the deck. Keep the 2 of
clubs on top where it started.

7 Pull a random card, then…

Is this your card? The 7 of diamonds?

No.

8 Throw the deck in anger at the
table. Stand in triumph when
victim sees the 2 of clubs.

How to Take Off Your Thumb

This is the fundamental body dismemberment skill. Before you learn how to break your neck (p. 200), bonk your head (p. 252), put your eye out (p. 308), or break your nose (p. 327), you need to learn how to take off your thumb. We're sorry, but it's a course requirement. See the illustrations for the step-by-step.

What your audience sees.

What you see.

The Broom and Water Scam

Water

Broom

Sucker

The next time you're in the kitchen, and there is someone there who needs something to do, try this.

1 Fill a plastic or paper cup with water.

2 Get up on the counter and press the cup to the ceiling.

3 Ask your victim to get a broom and hold the cup to the ceiling while you get down.

That's it. You're done. Now you can wander off. What are they going to do? (Except maybe wonder why it is they ever do anything you ask them.)

How to Take Off Your Thumb Again

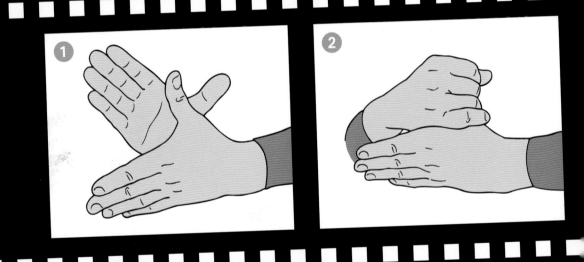

Seen from the front

We have no respect for a person who can only take their thumb off one way. Shows a total lack of immaturity.

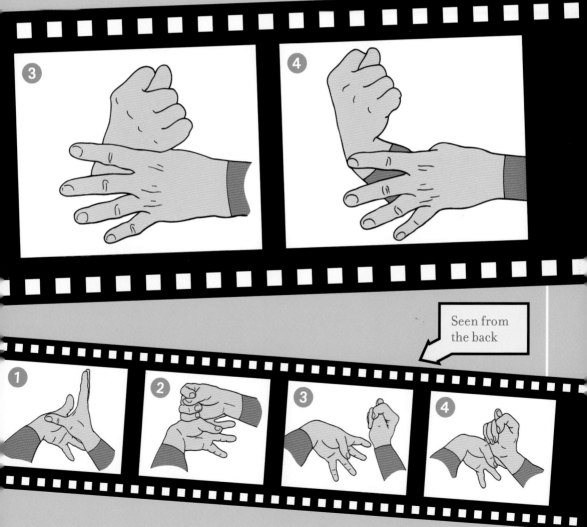

Seen from the back

Snorting Rubber Bands

Another bit of no-practice magic, located in the Eeeeuuuw Category. You'll need a rubber band and a nose.

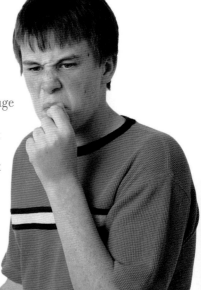

Oink!

1 Hook rubber band over pinkie. Stretch it and hold by your nose. Smile.

2 Make a huge snorting noise. Let the band snap back into your hand.

3

Cough and
let the band
hang out.

Lame magic
Power Straws

One of the key rules in Lame Magic is to play it big. The skinnier the trick, the fatter you'd better make the story. For example, if you sit at a table, place two straws side by side in front of you, and blow on them, they will roll apart from each other. And absolutely no one will care.

BUT. HERE IS A FAR BETTER WAY…

Carefully select the two straws from the entire collection available. Then sniff them, kiss them, hold them to the light, pass them around for inspection while you mumble a Tibetan prayer.

Then, during a moment of intense silence, set them both reverently on the table while you bow your head over them and simultaneously request everyone else at the table to begin chanting in unison: "OMMMMMMMMM."

Place your hands gently on the table and carefully, hypnotically, stroke the table while quietly asking everyone to gradually raise the volume of their mysterious chant.

Incredibly, slowly, *the straws will begin to move on their own,* rolling away from each other and towards your fingers, drawn like cobras out of their baskets, while everyone stares disbelievingly at them (and not you) as you purse your lips and silently, secretly, slimily blow on them.

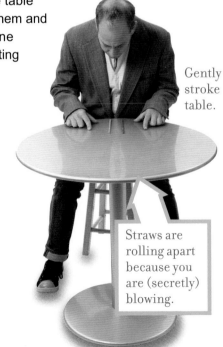

Gently stroke table.

Straws are rolling apart because you are (secretly) blowing.

How to Curve a Wiffle® Ball

Serious Wifflers throw at least four or five different kinds of pitches, but the curve is probably the bread and butter. The photograph shows the way a righty grips it, with the holes facing third base. (Southpaws? Holes face first.) Keep your fingers off the holes. Line up the middle finger and thumb on the seam.

You don't need a lot of speed for the curve, nor do you need to give it any special spin. Anything faster than a lob will curve. In fact, some pitchers get better effects when they go fairly slow. You can actually throw just behind the batter, and the ball will curve across the plate once you start getting the hang of it.

Important point! Don't use new! You want a scuffed-up ball. The new ones don't have nearly as much movement. Once you get a good ball, hang on to it. Each one is a little different.

By the way, there are lots of serious Wiffle® Ball players, and lots of organized tournaments. As usual, check out the Web for the local teams near you.

Holes facing
third base line.

How to Juggle

Juggling is one of those things that looks hugely harder than it is. This is fortunate since if it were otherwise we could never have learned how and it wouldn't be in this book.

Some kids learn to do a few jugs in 20 minutes; others take a couple of hours. On the **Klutz Universal Difficulty Scale,** juggling probably ranks a 4 out of 10 (where 1 is tying your shoes and 10 is learning the piano). Even so, here's an age warning: jugglers younger than 9 or 10 are the exception.

Learning how to juggle is something best done in small bites — 10 minutes here, 10 minutes there. But rest assured, if you keep trying, you'll get it.

Equipment: The basic rule is *Don't use tennis balls.* In fact, for beginners, balls of any kind are a pain because they bounce and roll under the couch. If you have to use balls, stand over a lawn. (Actually, a bed is the best — almost waist-high and balls won't roll; worst choice is a hard floor.) We recommend filling small socks with rice and using a rubber band to close them up. Once you learn how, of course, you can juggle with anything from tennis balls to flaming chain saws.

1 **The Drop.** Hold all the bean bags at waist height and drop them. Lean over, pick up and repeat. Since you're going to be dropping for the rest of your juggling life, you might as well learn proper technique. Take pride in your drops.

The key skill. How to toss one bag.

2 After you've practiced your drop enough, put two bean bags away. With the third one, toss it back and forth. Each toss should be about head high and should land right in your hand. Juggling is the art of great tosses — not great catches. If you have to reach or lunge for your tosses, keep practicing. In an ideal world, you could close your eyes and each toss would hit you right in the hand. (Call your hands "targets" to give you the right idea.)

Your target is the palm of your catching hand. Ideally you could close your eyes and still make the catch.

Tossing Two Balls

Get ready to go…

…up with one….

…up with the second. *But don't toss it until the first has peaked.*

3 When you're ready, pick up a second bag. You are about to learn the basic move, really the only move you'll need for basic three-bag juggling. Visualize how this goes. Up from one hand goes a perfect head-high toss. A beat later, just as the first toss starts down, the second bag zips by it, on the same head-high flight plan, just reversed.

You do NOT throw the two bags simultaneously (the chaos option), and you do NOT toss the first bag and then get rid of the second one just by sneaking it over to your other hand (the cheat option).

The two no-no's

Chaos

The Cheat

Do NOT toss the bags simultaneously.

Do NOT toss one and then hand the other over.

WHAT <u>SHOULD</u> HAPPEN VS. WHAT <u>DOES</u> HAPPEN

Unfortunately, we do not live in an ideal world, and you will probably cheat or create chaos on your first couple of efforts. Relax. Look at the pictures and breathe deeply. As the first toss goes up, say "UP." A moment later, toss the other bag from the other hand and say "UP" again. So it goes: "UP… and… UP."

④ Take a break. Go at it again some time later. And remember your mantra: "UP… and… UP."

⑤ Switch hands. If you can work with two bags, doing your "UP… and… UP" pretty well, then it's time to reverse it. If you've been starting with your right hand, start with your left and do that until it feels natural.

Switch hands.

Get ready to go…   …up with one.   Don't toss the second until the first has peaked.

Holding three balls. An emotional big step.

6 **The Jug.** If you're comfortable with two bags, and semi-comfortable starting with either hand, then pick up the third bag. This feels like it ought to be The Big Step, but it's actually not. That was The Toss. You're already over The Big Step.

Stop and think for a second about how this is going to look. Starting with your two-bag hand, you'll toss a bag up on a perfect little arc, head high and dropping right onto your other hand.

But before it lands, you'll clear that hand with a second toss (UP… and… UP) that looks just like the first, only in reverse. So far, all of this should be familiar territory.

Now comes the new thing. Except it's not. As the second bag tops out and starts dropping in, you'll toss the third bag right by it, on another little head-high arc. So now the mantra becomes "UP… and… UP… and… UP." The third toss is identical to the second, just from the other hand.

The Jug

Up with one.

Don't toss the second until the first has peaked.

Don't toss the third until the second has peaked.

Dirty little secret.

You've got two hands and three bags. Do the math. You only need to keep one bag in the air while holding two. Everybody talks about keeping three things in the air when they're juggling — urban myth. Juggling with three bags means keeping only one in the air. (That's why we were able to learn, and that's why most photographs of jugglers look like this. One in the air, one in each hand.)

7 Congratulations. It might take 10 minutes, it might take a few hours, but you'll eventually get the "UP… and… UP… and… UP" thing down. That's called a Jug. For a while, you'll be throwing everything out away from you and you'll be lunging and running after all your weird throws. But if you keep at it, you'll start to calm down and relax. Once you can do a single, controlled, non-panic Jug, take it one step further, the Jug-and-a-half: "UP… and… UP… and… UP…and… *UP*."

After you can do a Jug-and-a-half, that's four tosses. Go for five. Six. Seven. Each one is identical to the last. Juggling is an endless chain of great tosses and simple catches, linked together. Of course, there's a world of fancy tricks out there and once you think you're ready, we might recommend a book called *Juggling for the Complete Klutz* (try klutz.com or any bookstore).

Teh Cas Aginst Gud Spelg

Aoccdrnig to rscheearch at Cmabrigde Uinervtisy, it deosn't mttaer in waht oredr the ltteers in a wrod are. The olny iprmoatnt tihng is taht the frist and lsat ltteer be in the rghit plcae. The rset can be a taotl mses and you can sitll raed it wouthit a porbelm. Tihs is bcuseae the huamn mnid deos not raed ervey lteter by istlef, but the wrod as a wlohe. Amzanig, huh?

Shiw Tihs Two Yur Tchr!!!

356

How to Ruin a Nice Book

This is like one of those fake ink stains you can get at the magic shops. But it's free, works just as well, and for all you lazy types out there, it takes about 5 seconds! How perfect is that?

Tear a little strip of paper out of this page where it says to. Or you can use regular paper if you don't want to tear up a page.

1 Fold it in half where it says to.

2 Lick the back of it.

3 Stick the wet half to the cover of an expensive book. The other half should curl off the cover (see photo).

4 Leave on the coffee table and wait for a parent to notice. Won't they be thrilled!

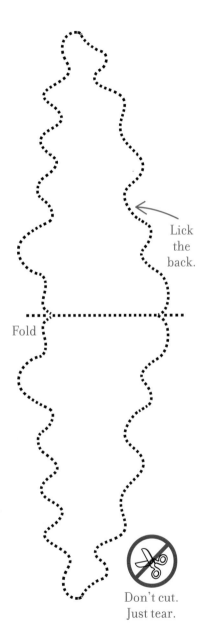

Lick the back.

Fold

Don't cut. Just tear.

How to Find Squirt Bugs

Squirt bugs are huge, nasty bugs that exist anywhere you might go swimming. Even the sink! You can catch them in your hand, and then, when you holler at someone else to come over and check it out, they will look into your hand, you will squeeze it and a jet of water will shoot into their face. ("…and THAT'S why they call them "squirt bugs"!)

1 You should be standing halfway in the water (unless you're at the sink, in which case just stick your hand in the water halfway). Look at the illustration. Your hand is mostly closed, but not completely. Your "bottom" fingers (pinkie, ring, middle) should be open, not quite touching your palm.

2 Call in your friend. Tell them you have a gross bug in your hand. When they come, make them lean over and peer into your hand. Then, all you do is…

3 …squeeze!

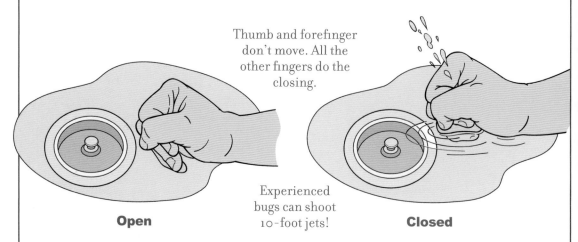

Thumb and forefinger
don't move. All the
other fingers do the
closing.

Experienced
bugs can shoot
10-foot jets!

Open

Closed

Yo-Yo 101

How to Walk the Dog

If you only learn one yo-yo trick in your whole life, Walking the Dog is it. You'll need to learn how to throw a hard sleeper that lasts 4 or 5 seconds. With the sleep time, you'll roll your yo-yo along the floor until just before it runs out of steam, at which point you'll give it a quick jerk and up it will pop.

Here are the instructions, tried and true.

You'll need a decent quality yo-yo (like the one we sell at klutz.com, for instance), but as long as you have a plastic yo-yo that sleeps, you should be all right.

We'll start with The Power Throw and Sleeper, the fundamental act of yo. Put the yo-yo up by your ear. Bring it down hard *but release it the instant you start your motion.* If it pops back up, chances are you didn't release soon enough. It's the most common problem.

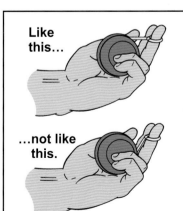

Like this...

...not like this.

Holding Yo-Yo at the Ready

Hold the yo-yo in your hand palm up with the string wrapped so it comes off your middle finger and goes over the top of the yo-yo as shown.

Still not sleeping? Throw your yo-yo hard, starting by your ear, and release instantly. If it still won't sleep, let it hang and unwind. Sometimes the string gets too tight. Give your yo-yo a minute to come to rest. Then wind it up and try again. In the worst cases, you'll get a knot inside your yo-yo. If you have that kind of luck, you'll have to take your yo-yo apart. The good ones come apart by unscrewing; the bad ones mean you're looking for a better yo-yo.

The number two problem? It sleeps, but you can't pop it back up. You're not throwing hard enough. Check out the illustration and really throw it down.

THE POWER THROW
Throw it hard and release it soon.

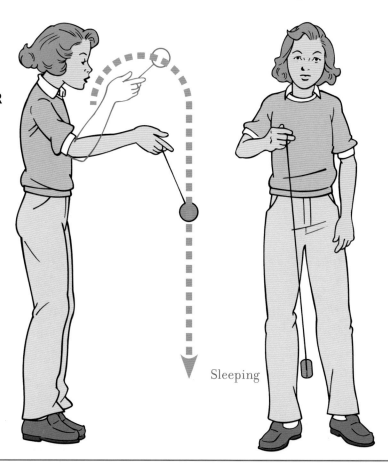

Sleeping

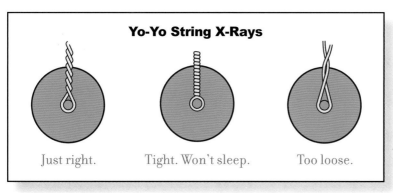

Yo-Yo String X-Rays

Just right.　　　　Tight. Won't sleep.　　　　Too loose.

Alternatively, you're throwing hard but it just pops back up, even though the string is loose enough. Try "softening" the throw. When your yo-yo hits the bottom, try to give a bit as it hits. It's a touch thing that comes with practice.

THE DREADED LEANER

This happens all the time. The yo-yo hits the end of the string and stops quickly because it leans against it. Solution? Throw accurately, directly over the top.

WHAT IF IT NEVER SLEEPS NO MATTER HOW MUCH YOU "SOFTEN" THE JOLT?

Then your string probably needs adjusting. No problem. Let your yo-yo hang until it stops spinning entirely. Then try again.

How to play
Tabletop Football

What follow are the official, no-more-arguments-ever-again, Klutz-sanctioned Tabletop Football Rules. Listen up.

First, fold your football out of a regular sheet of notepaper following these instructions.

1 Fold on the dotted lines until you get down to just the `tail.`

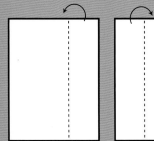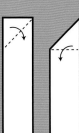

2 Tuck the tail inside the football. We've colored it `red` to help you see it.

Next, sit across the table from your opponent and shake hands.

Then, place your football within a hand's span of your edge and thump it so it goes spinning towards your opponent. Only three things can now happen:

1. It goes too long, dropping over the edge. Your turn is over.

2. It goes too short (meaning it does not overhang your opponent's edge). Your turn is over.

3. It lands just right, overhanging the edge of the table. Touchdown and six points for you! Score an extra point by thumping the football through your opponent's goalposts. You have to set up within a hand's span of your edge.

An overhang is a point.

QUARTER BALL

When you don't have a regulation football, we just use a quarter, or in desperate restaurant circumstances, sometimes the salt shaker. Just make sure you catch it in your lap when it goes long.

How to Make a Big Bang Bag

If you know how to do it, you can mix baking soda and vinegar in a plastic sandwich bag and get the thing to blow up making a nice little mess and a good-sized bang. Here is how it goes. (You probably ought to be working outside.)

INGREDIENTS

a plastic Ziploc® sandwich bag that doesn't leak (A lot of them do. Test by filling with some water and hanging upside down. If it leaks, it's a reject.)

piece of toilet paper

1 tablespoon vinegar

1½ tablespoons baking soda (baking powder doesn't work as well)

The simplest thing to do actually doesn't work. You can't just dump the vinegar in the bag, then the baking soda, seal it and run. The reason is the fizzing starts happening before you can get the zipper shut. Trust us. We've tried.

Folded Paper Packet System

Here's how to buy yourself enough time to seal the bag before it blows.

1 Start by dumping the baking soda in the middle of a piece of toilet paper and fold it up carefully into a packet.

2 Then, put the vinegar in the plastic bag.

3 Next, hold the packet inside the bag away from the vinegar while you seal with the other hand. Slick.

4 Finally, drop the packet into the vinegar, put the bag on the ground and back away. You usually have about a minute, depending on how well you folded your packet.

Hold baking soda up and away from vinegar while sealing bag.

Baking soda inside folded piece of toilet paper, which is held inside sandwich bag.

How to Spin a Basketball on Your Finger

Call this a *10-Minute Miracle*. That's usually all it takes, although we really recommend you learn in short — unfrustrating — 3-minute lessons. Ten minutes of abject failure is more than we can usually take at one sitting.

1 Launch the ball with two hands and spin it hard. Key fact: You're not throwing the ball up, you're spinning it. Don't go for height, go for RPM's.

2 Immediately slide your (bent) finger under the middle of the ball. We don't use our fingertip, we use our fingernail. It's a bit more forgiving.

3 Keep your finger flexible, not stiff, and concentrate on staying dead center. The faster the spin, the easier this trick is. If you can put a broom on your palm, bristles in the air, and wander around the front yard keeping it vertical, you've got all the skills you'll need.

4 Advanced work: Once you can keep it on your finger for a few seconds, you can extend your act almost forever by slapping the ball with your hand to keep the spin going. But don't get too greedy. You won't be needing this step until you've had an hour or so of frustrating drops.

The One Big Secret? If you have to catch the ball on your fingertip, that means you've tossed it into the air like we told you not to. See step 3 again. No catching! Slide the finger into place!

When a ball dreams, it dreams it's a...

Frisbee®

A well-thrown Frisbee is a thing of magic and beauty and nobody should venture forth into the world without knowing how to manage the basics of Frisbee. We'll cover two kinds of throws — forehand and backhand. But this is just a taste. The world of flying discs is truly enormous and you should check out some of the online videos of freestyle and Ultimate to get some idea of what today's players can do. If you've only seen front-yard toss and catch, you will not believe what you've been missing.

The Backhand. This is the basic throw, although far from the only one. Everyone has the same problem with it — call it "the roll and dive syndrome."

Instead of a long flat throw with a nice hover at the end, the throw leaves your hand and quickly starts to roll over to a crash landing. Very common, very discouraging.

The crash landing. Cause? Letting go of it too late.

The biggest secret? Let go sooner. Everyone likes to hang on to the disc too long, especially when they're trying for distance. Practice with someone nearby, practice on a day with no wind, and practice releasing sooner than you think you need to. Look at the illustrations for the idea. Start small with 25-foot tosses. Do NOT start throwing long until you can successfully throw short. Build up your distance slowly.

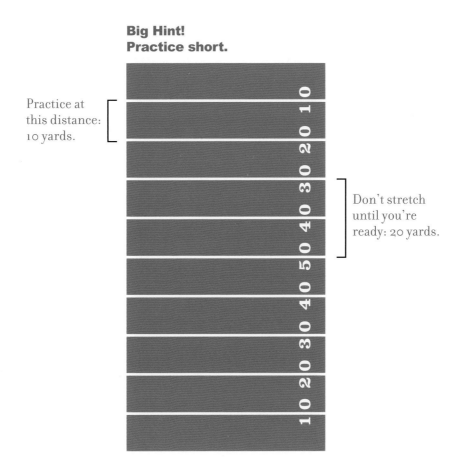

Big Hint!
Practice short.

Practice at this distance: 10 yards.

Don't stretch until you're ready: 20 yards.

THE BACKHAND

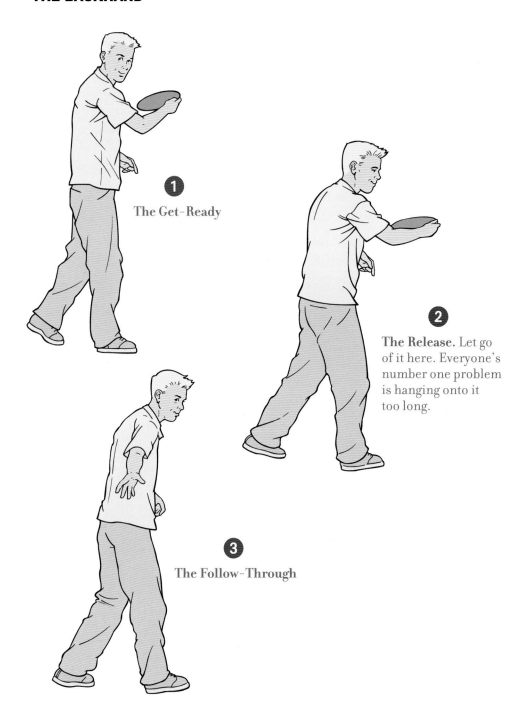

1
The Get-Ready

2
The Release. Let go of it here. Everyone's number one problem is hanging onto it too long.

3
The Follow-Through

BACKHAND GRIPS

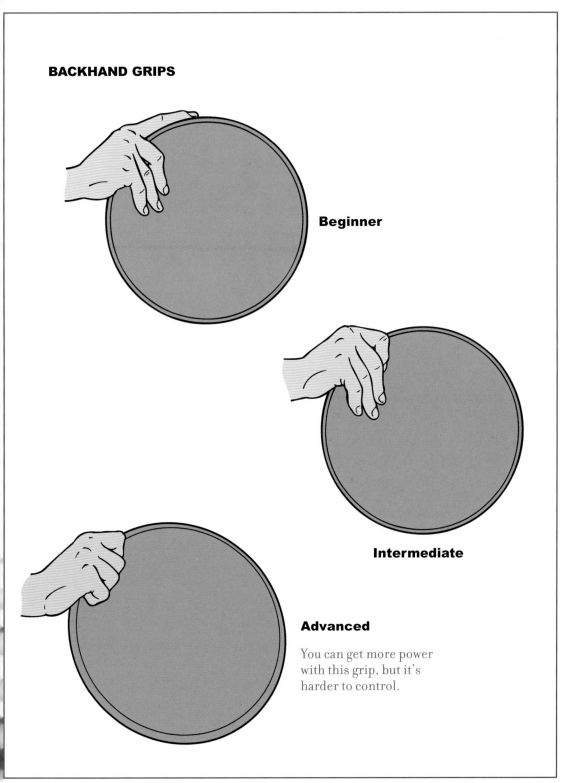

Beginner

Intermediate

Advanced

You can get more power
with this grip, but it's
harder to control.

THE FOREHAND

The forehand Frisbee throw is one of
the top ten skills in this encyclopedia.
It's a great throw — accurate, quick
and powerful.

1 **The Get-Ready.** Let the
disc droop just a little.
When it leaves your hand,
it should go out dead flat
for a short throw. As you
add power let it droop
on the release.

90% of
your power
is in the
wrist.

2 **The Release.** Sorry to sound like a cliché, but it's
all in the wrist, almost 100%. You could throw a
decent forehand with your upper arm tied to your
side with a belt. If you've ever been in a towel fight,
you've already learned the snap motion.

3 There is almost NO follow-through.
Close your eyes and pretend the
Frisbee is a towel you're going to
snap, or a whip you're going to crack.

THE FOREHAND GRIP

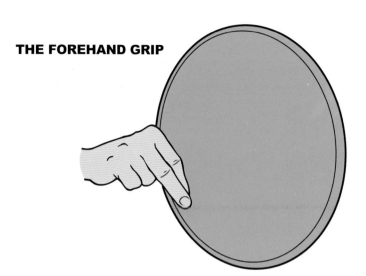

What will happen the first time you try? The disc will roll and dive, usually in front of you, although we have seen times when it's actually gone behind the thrower. If you can get your first forehand to land in front of you, call yourself an advanced beginner.

How hard is it? If you start with little 10-foot throws, you'll be getting some success within minutes. Use your wrist entirely. No arm at all.

The problems will begin when you start getting cocky and going for too much distance too soon. Solution? Keep it short. Focus on the wrist snap. Stretch your throws slowly, back up one step at a time. As soon as the disc starts to roll and dive, get closer again unless you love the experience of retrieving bad throws.

With more experience, you'll add some "arm" and release the disc at an angle, not flat. But don't get ahead of yourself. Walk before you run.

Or snake

How to Train an Attack Rat

Although these instructions here are written for rats, they work just as well for any other kind of animal as long as it's a good-looking fake toy one.

1 Tie long thread to fake rat.

2 Place on sidewalk or in hallway. Hide in bushes or behind door or furniture.

3 As people approach, begin to tug on thread.

Getting ready.
Adult approaching,
fake rat on string.

How to Make Radio-Controlled Underwear

After you get tired of playing with one of your radio-controlled cars, you should think about some modifications. Here's one.

1 Find underwear.

2

Tape a box…

3

…to a radio-controlled car.

4

Like this.

5

Put underwear…

6

…on box.
Done.

Better answers for your answering machine

Hello?

Since your answering machine only gets to say one little thing, we'd like to suggest that you make it a little special thing. Delete that boring message you have on it right now and replace it with something that has a little more zing to it. Like one of these...

Hi! We're actually at home right now, screening our calls. Leave a message and if we pick up, you're someone we want to talk to. If we don't pick up... well, can you say "hint"? [beep]

[Start this message normally, but as it goes on, do it slower... and slower... and slower... with more and more pauses.] Hi! This is the... answering machine. But I'm running low on... batteries. I'll try to remember your message, but I'm... scared and it's getting... very... dark. *[beep]*

Hi! We're not here right now, but if you'll just leave a message on our new machine here. [pause] Come on, machine, let's hear that beep. C'mon. Just a little one. You can do it. That's it. C'mon boy. That's it. [pause] OH, COME ON, FOR CRYING OUT LOUD! BEEP YOU STUPID MACHINE! *[beep]*

Hello? [pause] *Hello?* [pause] **Hello!**

I can't understand a word you're saying. [pause]

You're mumbling!!! [pause]

Now you're breaking up. [pause]

Can you turn down the music? [pause]

Oh, *NEVER MIND!* Just leave a message at the beep. *[beep]*

How to Do Cat's Cradle

A lot of the cat's cradle string figures can be done solo. But the game Cat's Cradle needs two people (or one person with four hands). Here is the way we teach it in our own immortal Klutz book, *Cat's Cradle*®, by Anne Johnson. Two shoelaces tied together make a nice cat's cradle loop. Or you can order a multi-color, deluxe loop from us at our Website, klutz.com.

You'll need a string about a yard long. Tie it in a loop. Two shoelaces tied together work well.

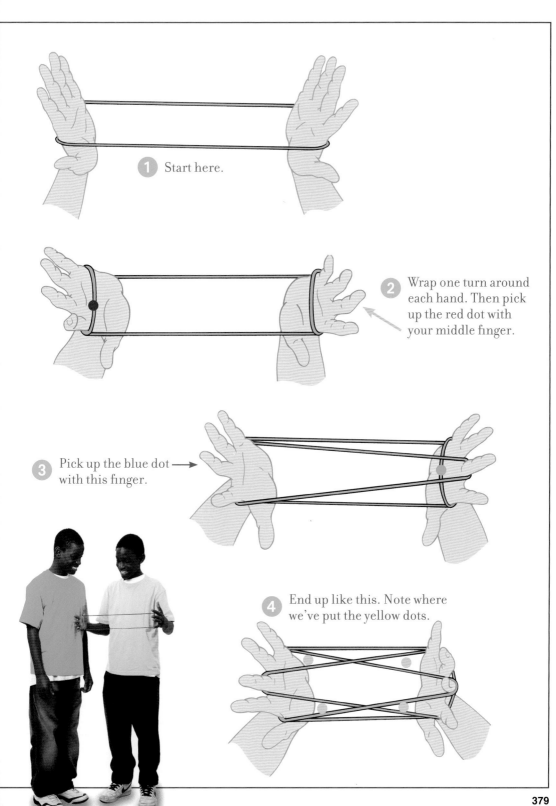

1 Start here.

2 Wrap one turn around each hand. Then pick up the red dot with your middle finger.

3 Pick up the blue dot with this finger.

4 End up like this. Note where we've put the yellow dots.

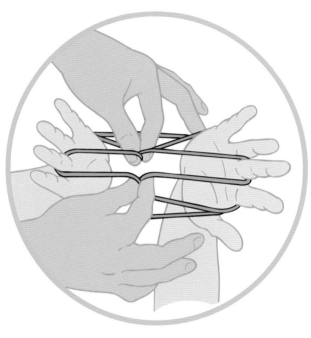

5 Pinch the strings where we've put the yellow dots. See previous page.

6 Keep pinching and pull out from the top. Note where we've put the red square.

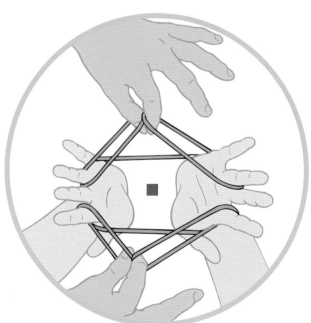

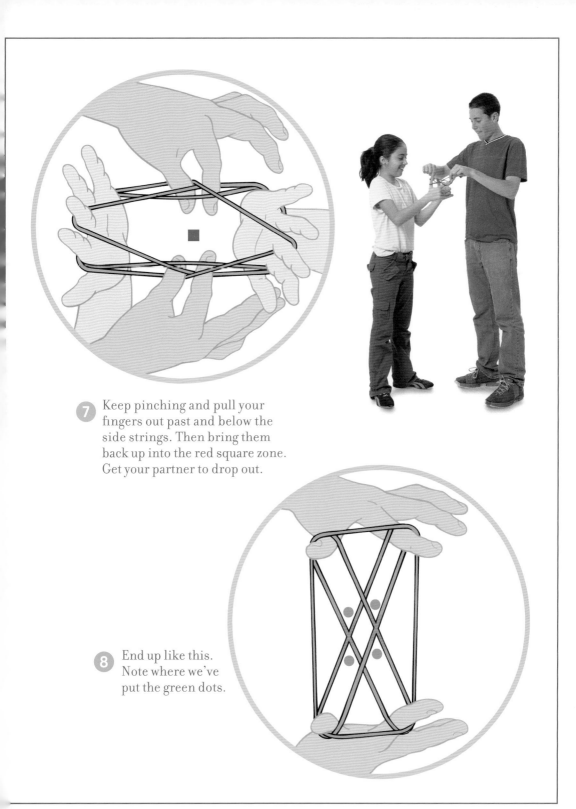

7 Keep pinching and pull your fingers out past and below the side strings. Then bring them back up into the red square zone. Get your partner to drop out.

8 End up like this. Note where we've put the green dots.

The next four steps will make **Candles**.

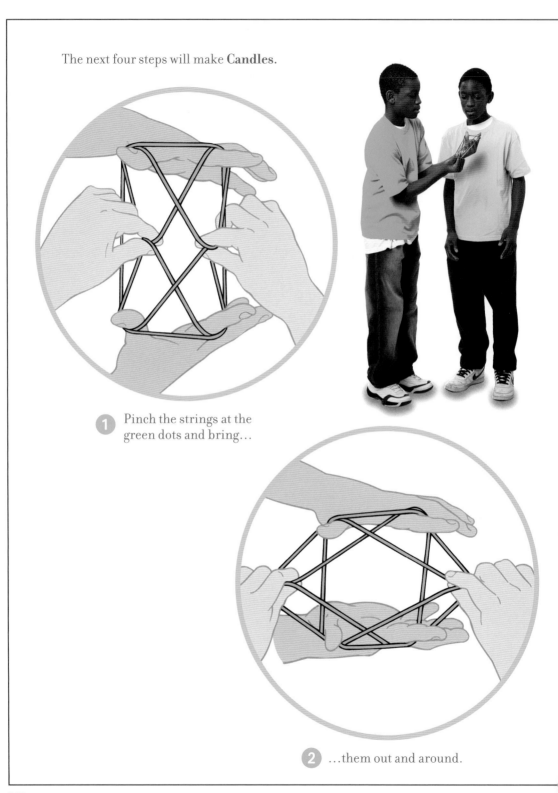

1 Pinch the strings at the green dots and bring...

2 ...them out and around.

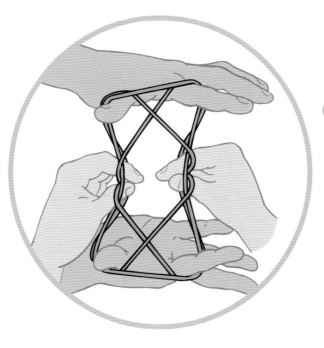

3 Now bring them back into the middle. Get your partner to drop out.

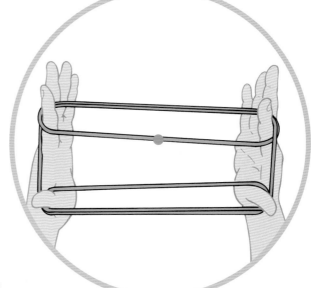

4 End up like this. Note where the green dot is.

End of Candles.

The next five steps will make **Manger**.

1. Pick up the green dot with your pinkie, the red dot with your other pinkie.

2.

3. Stick your thumb and index finger into the purple squares. Hang onto strings with pinkies.

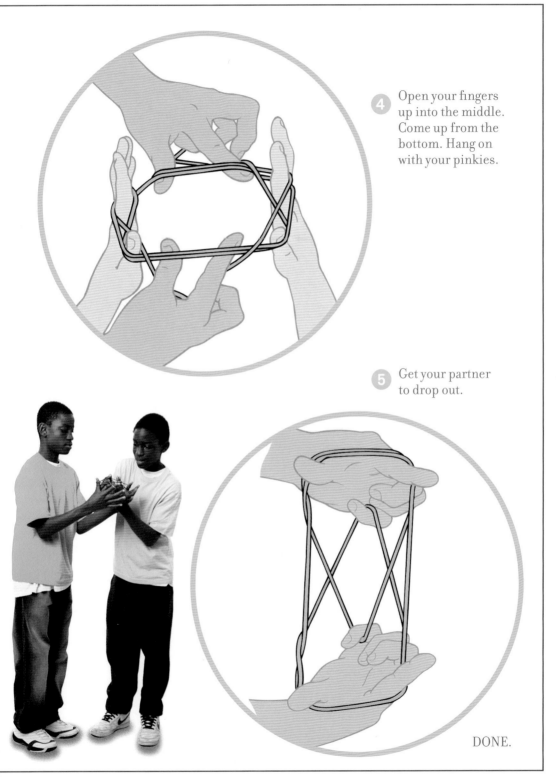

④ Open your fingers up into the middle. Come up from the bottom. Hang on with your pinkies.

⑤ Get your partner to drop out.

DONE.

How to Build a Domino Chain with Books and Junk

The current world record for a domino chain is a little under 4 million. If you would like to challenge that record, we wish you well and you should probably get started now if you want to finish before you die.

On the other hand, if you would like to build a domino chain out of books and junk that you can then use to knock down a big tall tower of books — look no further, here are the instructions. Or at least the inspiration. Since you'll be using your own stuff, you'll have to modify appropriately. Please do.

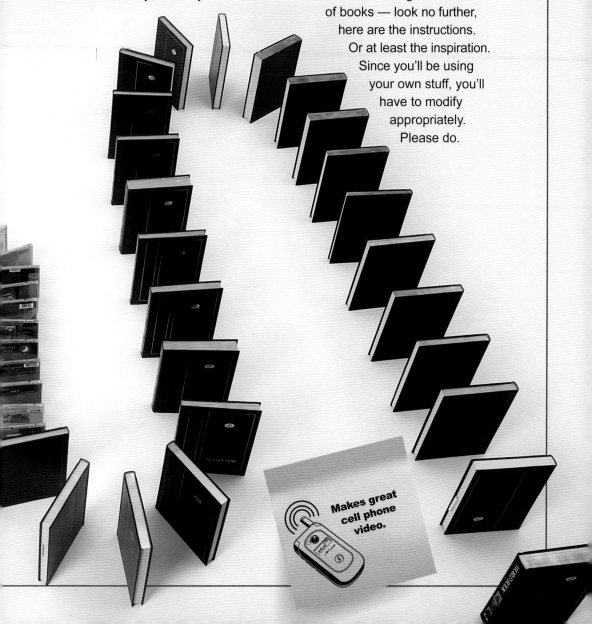

Makes great cell phone video.

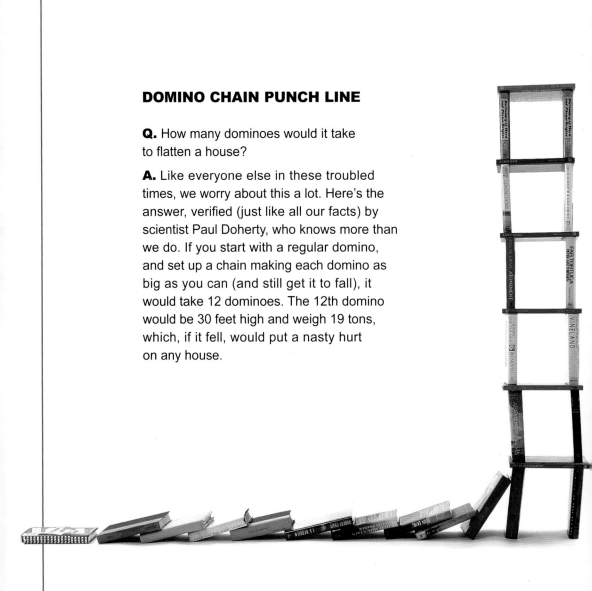

DOMINO CHAIN PUNCH LINE

Q. How many dominoes would it take to flatten a house?

A. Like everyone else in these troubled times, we worry about this a lot. Here's the answer, verified (just like all our facts) by scientist Paul Doherty, who knows more than we do. If you start with a regular domino, and set up a chain making each domino as big as you can (and still get it to fall), it would take 12 dominoes. The 12th domino would be 30 feet high and weigh 19 tons, which, if it fell, would put a nasty hurt on any house.

Pop quiz
your parents again

What Slimy Thing in Your Head Is Shaped Like This?

Actual Size

Here's another pop quiz for parents and other grown-ups who think they know so much because they have so much more "experience." Show them this picture and then let them "think" for a while, before you finally tell them the answer, which is, incidentally, *eyeball*.

Play Superball-verang

This is probably the coolest thing you can do with a SuperBall®.

1. Find a table. The underside should be flat and smooth. Stand away from it a few feet.

2. Throw the superball fast to the ground so it bounces off the ground and then hits the bottom of the table hard.

3. The superball will then reverse course and bounce back off the floor and right back to you. (Trust us, it will.)

With a little bit of practice, you can actually close your eyes, and it will bounce right back into your hand. Sometimes.

Tennis ball in tube sock.

Play Schmertz Ball

If you think of a ball as a flying dot, a schmertz is a flying dash. You make a schmertz by putting a tennis ball into a tube sock and knotting off the end of it.

You **throw** a schmertz by swinging it round and round and letting go.

You **catch** a schmertz by the sock, not the tennis ball.

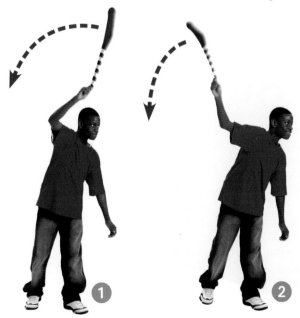

1 Swing…

…swing…

3 …and release.

How to Do the Deadly Selfnap

A friend of ours gave us this little bit. Her father, she says, would always use it as his exit after telling them their goodnight story when she was little.

"Traumatized me for years," she said.

Good night, kids.

Flatland tricks

How to Do a Wheelie

The road to BMX greatness is long, bumpy and littered with the occasional broken bone. But if you would like to check it out, or at least the first few steps, then you need to learn how to do a wheelie. It is step one on the BMX Path.

How hard is a wheelie? Getting the front wheel to pop off the ground — and then pop right back — is pretty easy. Maybe 10 minutes. But getting yourself stable on the back wheel, and being able to pedal forward even for a few yards — that's a different matter. You should take the process in small bites, but figure a week or two of trying and failing.

Equipment: You don't have to use a BMX bike to do a wheelie. In fact, a mountain bike might even be a little easier. Ideally, you want to have a very short stem on the handlebars, and a high gear. Mountain bikes usually qualify on both counts.

You DO have to have a helmet since you WILL fall. If you have wrist guards, use them. Practice in a parking lot (or maybe even on a lawn) where you don't have to worry about cars.

First step? Learn how to get off the back in a hurry. You'll be doing it a lot, so you might as well get used to it and learn the safest technique.

Ride your bike slowly, straight ahead. Be in a high gear and, when you're ready, hit the pedals one hard stroke while you pull hard on the bars and shift your weight back.

The front wheel should come off the ground high and hard. As it does, hop off the back. Land on your feet; repeat as necessary.

After you've gotten used to the dismount, you can start the real process of learning.

1 Get back on the bike and get relaxed. Put one finger on the rear brake. Pedal forward slow and straight.

2 On the count of three, shift your weight back and pull up on the handlebars. DON'T use the brakes. Shift backwards on your seat and pedal at medium speed. Try to hit that magic balance point. Lay off the brakes for a while. It's not until you start pedaling more than a few yards that you'll start to "feather" the brakes. It's a good way to keep on the balance point. But for beginners, using the brakes is tough.

Find the magic balance point that you can hold.

1 One, two, three, one, two, three...

Drive your family batty

How to Play "Chopsticks"

4 One, two, three, one...

5 two ...

"hopsticks" is a piano version of a leaky faucet. It's a timeless tune that we're including here for two reasons: One, you can learn how to play the most celebrated musical instrument of them all, while simultaneously driving your parents and siblings batty! Two birds with one stone!

And repeat.

Bulletin Boardies

The next time you're snapping a shot of a friend, think ahead for a moment about what he or she will look like stuck to a bulletin board with a thumb tack. That kind of thing hurts. We suggest you plan for the pain.

Just for practice, cut this photo out and stick to bulletin board.

Extreme Bill Makeovers

George Washington lived before cameras. As a result, nobody knows what he really looked like. All we have are painted portraits that are more or less guaranteed to be at least a little faked. (People who paint portraits for a living like to eat just like the rest of us. And if their portraits don't flatter their subjects, they won't.)

On the other hand, the portraits that we are providing here are photographic and brutally honest to their subjects. Trust us. We suggest you cut them out, and with the help of a glue stick, put some truth onto your currency.

And don't worry. You won't get arrested. Probably.

The Buttonhole Killer Pencil

Sam Loyd (1841–1911) is sometimes called the greatest puzzle brain who ever lived. He invented hundreds of puzzles including one that we're calling the buttonhole killer pencil. It is one of the classic mechanical puzzles of all time, like a ship in a bottle, but trickier.

Here's the way it goes. Tape a 2-foot length of string to a pencil. Congratulations. Now you have a pencil with a loop attached. The loop has to be an inch shorter than the pencil. The rule is you can't take the loop off. Ever.

Attach your looped pencil to a shirt or jacket through the buttonhole. You'll have to follow the directions to get this right. It's easy and very difficult. You'll see what we mean when you try it.

Give the shirt to anyone else with these instructions: Take the pencil off the shirt. You can't cut it off. You can't rip the loops off. You can't use violence or profanity in any way. When they finally give up, look at the instructions on the next page and show them how to do it.

This distance…

…is an inch less than this.

1 Start like this.

2 Unbutton shirt. Insert pencil through buttonhole and loop…

3 …like this.

4 Pull snug. The puzzle? Get it off.

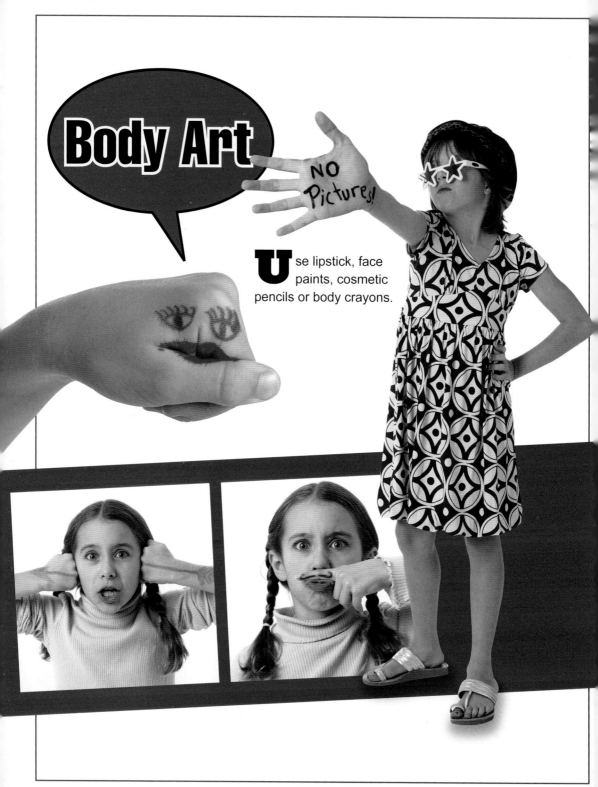

Body Art

U se lipstick, face paints, cosmetic pencils or body crayons.

How to Shrink Heads

Nothing looks nicer around your home or patio than a nice shrunken head. When guests are coming over, you can use it to brighten up a table setting, or hang it on the porch, like a wind chime from New Guinea. Here is the recipe.

Mix ½ cup lemon juice with 2 teaspoons salt in a bowl.

Next, carefully peel a largish apple. Keep the stem on while you roll it around in the lemon juice mixture. Then, carve out the eyes and mouth. Don't be shy about this since all your cuts will shrink quite a bit. Afterwards, wet it all again thoroughly.

Pull out the top rack of your oven and hang the apple from it using a short string tied to the stem. Slide the rack back into the oven and turn it on to its lowest setting for just a few minutes before you turn it off. Then don't do anything. Leave your apple hanging in the oven overnight.

Oven rack ➡
Apple ➡

In the morning, take it out and hang your head somewhere inside where it can dry for ten days and do its shrinking thing. If the stem breaks off, just replace it with a screw.

Answers

PAGE 11

Evett Mar Valaki Ebbol...

...az etelbol amit nekem kinalsz,
vagyen vagyok az elso?

means

Waiter, this meal you're serving me,
am I the first to eat it?

PAGE 22

A Vocab Quiz for Your Parents

DEFENESTRATE:
to throw out a window

CALLIPYGIAN:
possessing a big shapely rear end

STERNUTATE:
sneeze

COPROLITE:
fossilized dinosaur doo-doo

PHILTRUM:
the little groove that runs
between your upper lip and nose

SNOLLYGOSTER:
an unethical individual,
frequently a politician

GALLIGASKINS:
loose-fitting pants

ABSQUATULATE:
to leave in a hurry

PAGE 23

Bumper Stickers

RUGREST = Rutgers
MODERN EAT = Notre Dame
SIN IN COWS = Wisconsin
SNODFART = Stanford
FRIED CALF = Radcliffe
SCARYUSE = Syracuse
HAM ICING = Michigan

PAGE 44

What Color Are Blender Burgers?

☑ **B** ▮

PAGE 74

Try the World's Hardest 3-Piece Jigsaw Puzzle

PAGE 93

Decoder Badges

All the toilet seats were stolen from police headquarters. Now the police have nothing to go on.

Q: Where do you find a no-legged dog?
A: Right where you left him

Q: What do the letters DNA stand for?
A: National Dyslexic Association

Q: How much do pirates pay for their earrings?
A: A buccaneer

PAGE 110

Can $\frac{Stand}{U}$ This?

1. Sandbox
2. Man overboard
3. I understand
4. Reading between the lines
5. Long underwear
6. Crossroads
7. Downtown
8. Tricycle
9. Split level
10. Three degrees below zero
11. Neon lights
12. Circles under your eyes
13. High chair
14. Paradise
15. Touchdown
16. Six feet underground
17. Mind over matter
18. He's beside himself
19. A backward glance
20. Life after death
21. G.I. overseas
22. Space program
23. A long letter from home
24. Just between you and me

PAGE 110

Connect the Squares

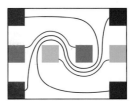

PAGE 118

Name That Doodle!

2. Spaghetti served by a very organized waiter.
3. A fly stuck in an ice tray.
4. A snowman with a pierced belly button.
5. A mouse hole with a doorbell.
6. A pig hiding around a corner.
7. Shark passing gas.
8. Overhead view of man with a bad comb-over.
9. A rollerblader on a skateboard.
10. Camel with a seatbelt.

Acknowledgments

Editor
John Cassidy

Design
Kevin Plottner

Illustration
Buc Rogers

Photography
Peter Fox
Liz Hutnick
Katrine Naleid
Paula Weed

Art Direction
Kate Paddock
Jill Turney

Production
DeWitt Durham

Help
Julie Collings
Theresa Hutnick
Dan Roddick
Michael Stroud

Production Design
Kayt de Fever
Rose de Heer

Editorial Assistance
Valerie Wyatt

Permissions
Marybeth Arago

More Help
David Barker
Laurie Bryan
Nathan Diehl
Paul Doherty
Susan Fox
Vicki Friedberg
Sherri Haab
Bill Harley
Georgia Herzog
Jenny Hsin
Barb Magnus
Gary Mcdonald
Daniel Miller
Bill Olson
Don Rathjen
Michael Sherman

Models
Ross Adams, Adlai Alexander, Jim Baer, Christine Barry, Shawn Barry, Chris Bates, Annie Bergquist, Nicole Berry, Travis Bowers, Dan Browne, Maya Bruhis, W. Scott Bryan, Davy Burke, Antwon Chatmon, Sean Chatmon, Tini Chorba, Bob Cullenbine, Ethan Davis, Nathan Diehl, Jennifer Donat, Mitch Donat, Bowen Doxee, Graham Fisher, Tup Fisher, Matt Fogarty, Hamish Forsythe, Christina Foung, Jenner Fox, Kaela Fox, Peter Fox, Susan Fox, Bryan Furlong, Dan Gilman, Gabriel Greening, Kathy Harrington, James Harrison, Jeff Harrison, Simon Hauser, Eric He, Jasmine Howe, Sean Hurlburt, Peggy Kelly, Carolyn Kramer, Richard Kramer, Kate Krislov, Lauren Kucik, Bernice Lazarus, Young Ju Lee, Jurgen Lew, Anthony Lim, Arne Lim, Stephen Lim, Blaine Marchant, Molly McAndrew, Gary Mcdonald, Daniel Miller, Hannah Min, E. Ulysses Morales, Bill Olson, Kael Price, Jim Sanchez, Josh Schneck, Ian Sims, Robert T. Smith, Ashvin Srinivasan, Cass Taylor, Corie Thompson, Eric Tracy-Cohen, Hannah Tuminaro, Jill Turney, Sergio Valente, Daisy Weed, Remi Wolf, Charlie Wolfson, Erik Young

Credits
Inside Front Cover: Banana © iStockphoto.com/Matt84. Page 12: Sneeze © Harold & Esther Edgerton Foundation, 2007, courtesy of Palm Press, Inc. Page 15: Orange © iStockphoto.com/Ljupco. Page 24: Pencil © iStockphoto.com/apletfx. Page 30: Fork © iStockphoto.com/tstajduhar; Paper © iStockphoto.com/blackred. Pages 32, 45, 56, 282: Quarter © iStockphoto.com/WebSubstance. Page 33: Tomb © iStockphoto.com/mbousquet. Page 40: Jet © iStockphoto.com/egdigital. Page 44: Blender © iStockphoto.com/kickstand. Page 44: Fly © iStockphoto.com/cezars. Page 45: Hand © iStockphoto.com/Bibigon. Page 51: Shark © iStockphoto.com/cdascher. Page 54: Cell phone © iStockphoto.com/yzak. Page 56: Steel © iStockphoto.com/da_kuk_work. Page 65: Ear © iStockphoto.com/hidesy. Pages 74–75: Puzzle cowboys (mules): © Mark Summers 1996. Page 77: Wood © iStockphoto.com/anzeletti. Page 83: Glass © iStockphoto.com/Matejay. Page 85: Bird © iStockphoto.com/marses. Page 86: Snail © iStockphoto.com/lucgillet. Page 88: Cherry © iStockphoto.com/pixelmaniak. Page 98: Paper © iStockphoto.com/spxChrome. Pages 100–101: Duct tape © iStockphoto.com/snapshot1329. Page 104: Elvis impersonator © iStockphoto.com/motorenmano. Page 106: Envelope © iStockphoto.com/DNY59. Page 109: Wood © iStockphoto.com/NNehring. Page 111: Biohazard illustration © iStockphoto.com/benoitb; Refrigerator © iStockphoto.com/gmnicholas. Page 117: Dollar © iStockphoto.com/Kuzma. Page 124: Broccoli © iStockphoto.com/kerioak. Page 136: Wrestlers, Jupiterimages/Ned Frisk Photography; © Image State-Pictor/Jupiter Images. Page 139: Pen © iStockphoto.com/Gambero. Page 145: Dinosaur: © Greg Epperson.

Can't get enough? Here are two simple ways to keep the Klutz coming.

1. Get your hands on a copy of The Klutz Catalog. To request a free copy of our mail order catalog, go to klutz.com/catalog.

2. Become a Klutz Insider and get e-mail about new releases, special offers, contests, games, goofiness and who-knows-what-all. If you're a grown-up who wants to receive e-mail from Klutz, head to www.klutz.com/insider.

If any of this sounds good to you, but you don't feel like going online right now, just give us a call at 1-800-737-4123. We'd love to hear from you.

More Great Books from Klutz

Card Trickery

Klutz Book of
Paper Airplanes

Juggling for the
Complete Klutz®

Battery Science

Draw the
Marvel® Heroes

LEGO® Crazy
Action Contraptions

The Solar Car Book

The Klutz Book
of Magic

Mother Nature Goes
Nuts!

The Outtakes

A great many things that we prepared for this book were cut as the editing process went on. Here are a few.

How to Throw Your Voice

How to Train Your Parents

How to Pick Locks

How to Win Snowball Fights

How to Annoy Your Sibling(s)

How to Do Banana Art

How to Lag Coins

How to Burp on Command

How to Write Your Own Riddles

How to Do Rope Tricks

How to Test Your Teacher

How to Win at Battleship

How to Tell Dumb Jokes

How to Fake a Temperature

How to Fool Your Cat

How to Win the Dessert Battle

How to Draw Comics

How to Talk Underwater

How to Make Real Rockets

How to Start the Hiccups

How to Be a Fake Ghost

How to Repeat Dreams

How to Make Your Foot Disappear

How to Slurp Spaghetti

How to Stand on Your Head

How to Win at Hide and Seek

How to Hypnotize People

How to Make Mashed Potato Castles

How to Launch Pumpkins

How to Do Cartwheels

How to Play Mumblety-Peg

How to Build a Backyard Dunk Tank